SAMANTHA of SAMARIA

A NOVEL

JOHN R. RAMSEY

© 2009 by John R. Ramsey. All rights reserved.

WinePress Publishing (PO Box 428, Enumclaw, WA 98022) functions only as book publisher. As such, the ultimate design, content, editorial accuracy, and views expressed or implied in this work are those of the author.

No part of this publication may be reproduced, stored in a retrieval system, or transmitted in any way by any means—electronic, mechanical, photocopy, recording, or otherwise—without the prior permission of the copyright holder, except as provided by USA copyright law.

Unless otherwise noted, all Scriptures are taken from the *King James Version* of the Bible.

ISBN 13: 978-1-60615-005-4
ISBN 10: 1-60615-005-7
Library of Congress Catalog Card Number: 2009923092

To all the strong women in my life:
my mother Virginia; my wife Brandy;
and my four daughters
Kimberly, Victoria, Kaeleigh, and Olivia.

Chapter One

THE SUN'S SLENDER rays pierced the crack in the weathered shutter, casting early morning light on the sleeping woman. Even in quiet repose, she bore around her closed eyes the tiny lines of a world-weary existence. As the sun continued its rise over the jagged edges of the nearby mountain peaks, the woman's neighbors awoke and began the routine of morning chores.

A short time later, the occasional sound of laughter and soft murmur of feminine voices passed outside the woman's clay hut. The women of Sychar, gracefully balancing water jugs on their shoulders and sharing tidbits of news, followed the well-worn path the half mile or so from the village to Jacob's well. They neither noticed nor cared that the woman didn't join them.

Eventually the sun rose high enough to send its light deep into the dim room. Samantha moaned and covered her face with a tattered wool blanket. Even that simple movement sapped her strength. Finally, the heat in the room increased until Samantha couldn't stand it any longer. With the slow movements of a hung-over drunk, she peeled the blanket from her body and sat up.

If only she were hung over. At least then there would be an explanation, a reason, for her lethargy. A minute passed and then another. Samantha took a deep breath and glanced behind her. The wooden bench was empty. In the stillness of the hot room, she listened for the telltale signs of someone lingering nearby. Silence. So he had gone. Why should she be surprised? Didn't they always leave? And wasn't it what she wanted?

Perched on the edge of the bench's straw mattress, Samantha tried to remember the events of the previous night. An argument, the words reverberating against the baked walls. A night like so many others. Sweeping her long dark hair away from her face, Samantha stood up and walked toward the water basin. A sharp pain shot up her foot and she hopped back to the bed. From her vantage point, she saw the clay shards lying on the floor. Of course. The lamp. She had thrown it at him. Had it hit him? Had he ducked? She shook her head. She couldn't remember.

Pulling a corner of the blanket from the bed, she wiped the small streak of blood from her foot. The shard had barely scratched the skin and the bleeding soon stopped. Samantha stared at the stained blanket. Gritting her teeth, she rolled it into an untidy ball and tossed it with all her strength. It fell, graceless, in a heap at her feet. *That's me*, she thought.

Chapter One

Through the heavy silence, she became aware of approaching voices. The village women were returning with their pitchers of water, ready now to begin the daily routine of cooking and cleaning. Samantha sighed with the weight of endless days, of the drudgery and regret that stretched before her. She sat quietly while the murmurs came closer. Through the shuttered window, she could distinguish the voices. Her nearest neighbor and the wife of the local tanner were engaged in a good-natured argument about the quality of the season's pomegranates.

What does it matter? Samantha wanted to shout at them. The round red fruit would be pulled, luscious and ripe, from the trees to be made into desserts and juices. The thick rind would be boiled, becoming yellow dye for their spun cloth. The same as every season that ever was and ever would be. A time of festivity for the women to gather and share the work. But not for Samantha. Her turn came later, after the others returned to their houses. Alone, she would gather the remaining pomegranates, the ones no else wanted.

In times past, Samantha had longed to be part of the chattering group, to share in the idle gossip, to join in the festivity of shared chores. But she had buried that desire long ago. Now she felt only annoyance at the cackling laughter that invaded her small world.

As the voices faded away, Samantha looked toward the window. Through the cracks, she could tell the morning had reached its peak. Now that the other women had returned to their homes, it was her turn to make the daily trek to Jacob's well. Alone.

That thought drew her gaze to the water basin and the jug that stood beside it. The pieces didn't match. The brown jug, ill-formed and pitted, was a common type. Samantha couldn't even recall where it had come from or how it had come to belong to her. The basin was a lovely piece of craftsmanship, smooth and well made. At one time, there had been a graceful pitcher of the same creamy tan shade. A fine, matched set. But the pitcher . . . Samantha shook away the memory. It was gone and she didn't care. Why should she care?

With slow movements, Samantha swept up the scattered pieces of the broken lamp from the packed earthen floor. Kneeling on one edge of the dropped blanket, she used it to sop up a small pool of olive oil that hadn't seeped into the ground. What a waste! She carelessly folded the blood and oil-stained blanket and dropped it in a basket that sat in a corner of the room. Later. She would take care of it later.

Samantha changed from her night shift to a faded but clean linen tunic, and wrapped her embroidered sash around her too-thin waist. She slid her feet into frayed leather sandals and tied the thongs around her skinny ankles. After brushing her thick hair with long, straight strokes, she pulled it back, properly, with a linen strip. Picking up a woven mat, a small pouch, and her veil, she opened the shutters and peeked out. No one was in sight. Good.

Stepping over the threshold, Samantha paused to let her eyes adjust to the harsh morning sun. Then she scurried across the empty courtyard and peered into the dimness of the pungent stable. The smell of sweet hay

Chapter One

mingled with stale manure. The cow was gone. So that was it. Memories of the previous evening trickled into her consciousness. She turned to the ladder that was leaning against the outer wall of the hut and climbed to the roof. With each rung, she cursed the poverty that kept her from repairing the nearby broken steps.

Standing on the roof, Samantha looked out over Sychar. She could see her neighbors, in their courtyards and on their roofs, engaged in morning activities. Several of the women worked in pairs as they ground the grain for the day's bread—another activity Samantha always did by herself. What respectable woman wanted Samantha's help? Or dared offer a helping hand of her own? And, of course, all of the women of the Samaritan town were respectable. All, except Samantha.

Even her hut, with its typical stone foundation and sun-baked clay walls, stood apart from the others. The small house sat on the outskirts like a poor relative whom no one wants to acknowledge. And yet, it was a good house, built long before Samantha was born by someone with an imagination. Most of the village homes had only two or three rooms, and the largest of those rooms served as the stable for the livestock. Samantha's house had two rooms, but her stable was a separate structure. The unusual setup gave Samantha a small measure of pride and the villagers an excuse for their resentment.

After surveying the other townspeople, Samantha retreated to the back corner of the roof. A ragged tent created a patch of shade, and Samantha dropped the mat in its center. Sitting cross-legged, she opened the pouch and pulled out a small mirror, a relic from a more prosperous time, though not a happier one. With a practiced hand and peering into the speckled mirror, she outlined her dark eyes with kohl. Samantha's performing this daily rite on her rooftop gave her neighbors yet another reason to gossip. Perhaps that's why she did it. Though no one could dispute that the sun provided more light on the roof than a dozen oil lamps inside the hut.

Finished, she carefully tucked the pouch, with the mirror and kohl inside, into the folds of her sash. She knew she should go for her water, but instead she continued to sit in the tiny patch of shade. She gazed southwest, across the plains to the rising peak of sacred Mount Gerizim. Samantha didn't mind the mountain in the mornings when the eastern sun revealed rocky crevices. But in the evenings, she couldn't abide it. Not when the mountain range cast its dreary shadow over the plain as the setting sun dipped below its highest peaks.

But those thoughts were for the end of the day. Right now the sharp images of the broken lamp and the soiled blanket pounded her head. Why did she have to remember? Why couldn't she just forget it all?

Chapter Two

David clenched his fists around the copper coins, fighting the impulse to throw them at the clerk's feet. But the money, though a paltry amount, was all he had. He didn't even want to think what Samantha would say when he returned home. David snorted. *Home?* That hovel wasn't his home. He didn't need to go there anyway. Why should he after she had flung that lamp at him last night? When he showed up with these few coins, she'd probably launch the lamp stand at him. Maybe he should go somewhere else. That would show her.

David swaggered away from the auction site, his back straight as a measuring rod. Wrinkles stretched across his forehead as he thought about the events of the previous night. After Samantha's outburst, he'd slept in the stable with the old cow. The animal's days were numbered once she dried up. Samantha raged at the poor beast. What had she said? "Around here, everything and everyone works for its keep. That means that cow, and if she doesn't have any more milk to give, then at least her old hide will be worth something."

"What's my hide worth?" David had asked in a failed attempt to tease Samantha into a better mood. But she only glared at him and climbed the ladder to the roof. David didn't follow her.

Instead he grabbed a threadbare blanket and stayed with the cow. This was where he had started out, and here he was again. As he tossed and turned, trying to find a spot of comfort in the scratchy hay, David thought about the early days with Samantha. When he first came to stay with her, she shared her evening meal with him, then pointedly retreated to her rooftop perch. He might wander through the village, but as the sky darkened into twilight, he returned to the stable. It was strange how the stable was disconnected from the main rooms of the hut. Yet it seemed fitting somehow for David's only shelter to be isolated from even Samantha's stony silences.

Later, the situation changed and David maneuvered his way into the hut and into Samantha's bed. But trying to sleep in the stable brought back all the dreary remembrances of trying to appease the hot-tempered woman who only gave him shelter because he owed her a debt.

During his restless night in the hay, David planned how he could restore himself to Samantha's good graces. This morning he rose early, up with the sun, and led the cow from the stable. The walk to the auction site was a long one, and David's mood alternated from sleepy resignation to subdued excitement as he dreamed of

Chapter Two

Samantha's reaction when he returned with enough copper coins to impress even her jaded spirit.

As David walked through the countryside, he began to notice the changes in the landscape. The desert floor, though violent and hard, had lost its battle to be impenetrable. Ragged weeds managed to pierce its rough, dry exterior. Scraggly green shoots broke through the resistance of the packed dirt. Thorns somehow managed to thrive. It seemed to David that even the rocks were multiplying as he wandered across one patch of extremely stony ground. The plants seemed at war with the desert, fighting for life in the humid heat.

At times, even the birds seemed to be working against the tender life. David watched as blue-black ravens swept down to scratch out and swallow the seeds scattered along the path. Eventually, David came to a small oasis. Here the scattered seeds had taken root and, nourished by a nearby spring, provided shade for the young man and the old cow.

"This is paradise," David said to the cow. He sat down beneath the shade of a multi-branched sycamore tree and pulled a handful of dried figs from his pouch. Stretching his long legs in front of him, David leaned against the tree trunk. Good ground like this was hard to find in the desert wilderness. He thought about the different types of ground he had seen since leaving Samantha's house. Dry ground, thorny ground, stony ground, ground attacked by birds. Only the hardiest weeds could really thrive under those conditions. But in this one spot, life exploded, green and abundant.

A quarter of an hour passed while the cow grazed and David considered the different types of soil. When his thoughts took him into a place he didn't want to go, he stood up and walked to the nearby wadi. He knelt and, cupping his hands, took a swallow of the cold, refreshing water. Sticking his head entirely into the stream, he let the water lift his dark wavy hair to the surface. For a brief moment, he felt the peacefulness of being in another world, one both familiar and strange. Sounds were muffled. The sun wasn't quite as hot. The wind was stilled.

When he came up for air, he shook his head and laughed as the droplets fell around him. "Why can't I be this patch of ground?" He looked at the cow and gestured at the grass at his feet. "Alive. Colorful."

Then he looked back over the ground they had walked before reaching the oasis. *That's who I really am,* he thought. Thorny ground. Caught in a web of responsibilities strong enough to hold him hostage, but not to support his ambitions. And why? What did he owe Samantha? How had she become his responsibility?

Merely thinking the question made him laugh. A sharp, dry chortle. What would Samantha say about that? He was sure that in her mind she thought it was the other way around. So how had he become her responsibility? The circular questions were enough to drive any man crazy. David turned his attention to the cow. Her long tail flicked the flies from her mangy brown hide as she stood quietly, nibbling at the tender shoots of the lush grass. From somewhere in the pit of David's stomach, he felt a knot of anger begin to grow.

Chapter Two

"Crazy cow," he muttered. "Don't you know where I'm taking you?" In a quick spurt of rage, he picked up a round pebble and flung it at her, but his aim went wide. "Can't even hit a cow." He leaned back again and shut his eyes. Is that what life was about? Like the cow? Being led to slaughter and not even knowing. Chewing the cud, flicking flies, never knowing that in a day or two a knife will be held to your throat. Surely there was more than that to life.

In a dour mood, David stood and brushed the loose dirt from his tunic. Twisting the rope attached to the cow's halter around the palm of his hand, he continued on his journey through the wilderness, though for David, the wilderness was not defined by terrain, but isolation. Whether the path was smooth or coarse, for David it was increasingly lonely. The decisions he had made before, the forks he had chosen to take, had placed him where he was today. Though he may have felt that the wilderness was waiting for him to stumble by, the truth was that he created it. A wilderness is an empty place. In this season of David's life, the wilderness stretched all around him.

Chapter Three

As the sun moved across the summer sky, so did the square of shade. For the second time that day, light pierced through Samantha's sleep. She awoke with a start and sat up, disgusted with herself for falling asleep on the roof. Shading her eyes with her hand, she peered into the sky. Noon. And still she had no water.

Samantha gingerly made her way down the steps from the rooftop. When she reached the broken ones, she jumped lithely to the courtyard floor. Back in the dark room, she adjusted her veil and placed her headdress over her waist-length hair. With the portable leather bucket and rope over one shoulder and the water pitcher poised on the other, Samantha began the hot, dusty trek to Jacob's well. Alone. Always alone. The empty jar was light compared to the heavy weight of the past that Samantha carried on her slender shoulders.

Chapter Three

Perhaps I'm destined to be alone, Samantha thought as she put one foot in front of the other. She thought back to her childhood, of hiding beneath a table with her brothers and sisters while verbal storms raged around them. Even as she comforted the youngest, she felt the mantle of loneliness descend upon her.

Then there were the nights when she awoke to hear her mother's muffled sobs. Samantha recalled sitting in the threshold of the small house throughout a long hot night as she waited for her father to come home. Praying for his return. Praying that the night would remain until he did. But the morning sun arose, shining indifferent heat upon the abandoned mother and children. *Where is he?* Samantha wondered, until it became a daily habit to consider the question, only to dismiss it from her mind. She didn't really care. He was just another hot-tempered lazy brute who blamed his wife and children for the disappointments life threw in his path.

As a young girl, Samantha learned to sleep with her wool blanket pulled partly around her head so both her ears were covered. The sound of her parents' arguments was never silenced by the childish gesture, but it was a way for Samantha to retreat into a small inner space deep within her spirit. With her ears covered and her mouth pressed into the thin mattress, her own nightmarish whimpers were muffled—or ignored by worn-out parents with too many mouths to feed.

In the dim memories of happier days, Samantha recalled flashes of her father's smiles. "My little bird," he called her as he bounced her on his knee or threw her, squealing into the air. "So like your mother." He was perfect then, this strong man who first laid claim to Samantha's tender heart. But as years passed and more children joined the family, it became harder to fill empty stomachs. The bright eyes lost their twinkle and became as hard as the worn path that led to Jacob's well. *Funny,* Samantha thought, as she looked at the dust kicked up by her sandals. *His eyes, the night he left for good, looked as scattered as these dust particles. But I didn't see it then. I thought he'd come back. I watched and waited for him to come back.*

He was the first of many. And now David was another to add to the list. She wondered where he was right now. Had he reached the auction yet? How much could he possibly get for that wretched cow? Samantha blinked away the momentary twinge of regret tugging at her heart. The cow had been with her a long time. Her words, spoken in anger, were coming to pass and she wasn't sure she liked it. But how could she blame David for taking her seriously? He probably thought he was doing her some grand favor.

Now she wished she had gotten up early. Why hadn't she stopped him? The cow might no longer give milk, but it had become a kind of companion. A chore that gave a rhythm, a structure, to her empty days. Perhaps the cow only needed a rest. Perhaps the milk would come again. Samantha laughed, dry and hoarse. Who was she kidding? And was she so lonely that a broken-down cow was the only friend she had? She kicked at a pebble in her path and watched it bounce ahead of her, tiny puffs of dirt marking its path.

Chapter Three

After her father left, Samantha vowed that she would never be like her mother. Never would she struggle to feed hungry children or lose her youth to the burdens of raising a family on her own. Her dreams were bigger than the small house where food was scarce and love even more so. Never would she resort to her mother's sordid means of gathering a few coins here and there. Samantha hated every one of the men who invaded her mother's rooms. Some stayed several weeks, others a few days or only one night. As the years passed, Samantha watched her mother grow old, and vowed a different life for herself.

Yet here she was, living in her mother's old hut with a man she hardly cared to know, not knowing when he would come and when he would go. Though the village was her childhood home, the other villagers scarcely spoke to her. Of course, they were more than happy to talk about her. And Samantha knew she gave them ample fodder for their idle tongues. She could leave, but she had nowhere to go. Unlike the father who took off after a drunken rampage and never returned, unlike the men who entered her life for a time only to disappear, Samantha had no choice but to stay where she was, a prisoner of her circumstances and of her gender.

The sun's heat intensified and Samantha chastised herself again for falling asleep on the roof. She should have gone for water as soon as the women returned instead of languishing on top of her house. Who did she think she was? A wealthy woman with maidservants to perform such mundane chores as fetching water? No, it was her lot to do for herself and she only had herself to blame that she was walking in the noonday heat toward Jacob's well.

As she often did on the lonely trek, Samantha found herself daydreaming about the long-ago patriarch whose name identified the precious well. Though Samantha's own genealogy was lost in the mists of history, almost all Samaritans shared in at least a small portion of the Hebrew heritage. Though she didn't know which of the twelve tribes birthed her own ancestors, she knew that the patriarch Jacob was the father of the twelve brothers from which the tribes descended, so she could certainly claim him as a distant father.

These were the kinds of thoughts Samantha kept to herself. How her mother would have laughed at Samantha's fascination with the Hebrew ancients. The woman only, ever, concerned herself with the day's troubles. "Don't go looking beyond today," she often warned her daughters. "There's enough trouble in these daylight hours without looking at tomorrow or thinking about the past."

Samantha didn't enjoy thinking about her future, or remembering her past. But neither was she content in the present. On these long treks to get water, she often dreamed of a past that existed hundreds and hundreds of years before she was born. For a short part of the day, she could put the present out of her mind and imagine herself in a different time.

What would it have been like to be Rachel? This was Samantha's favorite daydream. The beautiful younger daughter of the cheating Laban had captured the young Jacob's heart so completely that he worked fourteen years just to have her as his wife. Samantha knew from

Chapter Three

the village elders' stories that Rachel had had her own heartaches. For many years of her marriage, she was barren, unable to give Jacob the sons that were so important to a patriarch's household.

But surely even that sorrowful burden was lessened whenever Rachel found herself in Jacob's loving arms. Surely the love of such a man, one who had wrestled with an angel, was compensation for many burdens.

Though Samantha would never admit it to anyone, she sometimes imagined she was the lovely Rachel. Instead of going to Jacob's well to fetch water, she was going there to meet her beloved. Such dreams seemed to lessen the heat of the sun and the long, solitary distance to the well.

Today, though, Samantha found it impossible to get lost in her imaginings of another time. The memories of the previous evening were an impenetrable wall to any other thoughts or fanciful daydreams.

Despite her morning rooftop nap, Samantha felt exhausted as drops of sweat glistened on her forehead. Her own growing thirst kept her from falling along the dirt path in a heap as tangled and stained as the blanket she had tossed on her floor earlier that morning. One foot in front of the other. One more step. One more step. Life demanded that Samantha keep her misery alive just one more day.

Chapter Four

David had lingered too long at the quiet oasis, alternating between unreasonable anger and quiet contemplation. And his procrastination was going to cost him. At the auction yards, he handed the cow's lead to an overly eager young boy, unruly curls escaping from beneath his cap, who led her to a pen.

"How soon will it be before she's sold?" David asked the clerk.

The clerk, sitting on a stool in front of a small table, looked up at him. David saw the flicker of disgust in the man's eyes. But who had time for traditional greetings when there was money to be had.

"After the others," the clerk replied, his voice low and brusque. He turned back to his ledgers.

"But how long will that be?" David knew how to deal with insolent upstarts. The clerk's rudeness could not be tolerated.

Chapter Four

"I cannot say." The clerk didn't raise his head. "You will excuse me."

David kicked the nearby fencepost. Most of the buyers would make their purchases before the auctioneer ever made it to him. "It never fails," he shouted at no one in particular. "The little man is always last."

The other men turned toward him at the outburst. A few shook their heads in disgust, but most ignored him. Some had witnessed David's childish tantrums before, and no one felt obliged to engage him in conversation.

David walked a short distance from the others and folded his arms across his chest. Why couldn't they see that it wasn't his fault he was in this predicament? Had he even wanted to bring the cow to this stupid auction? No! Samantha had tricked him into doing it. He could have spent the day fishing or . . . well, something besides taking this long walk for nothing. It seemed the whole world was involved in some kind of conspiracy to make sure David was broke. "I never get a blessing," David muttered.

It wasn't that he hadn't tried. His head was full of plans, but something always happened. Just as the latest big deal was about to go through, a snag would tear the whole thing apart. Once he had dreamed of opening another auction just to have the satisfaction of shutting this one down. That would teach that simpering clerk a lesson he wouldn't soon forget. But for some reason, no one would loan him the money to get the venture off the ground. These people just didn't have any vision.

On a different occasion, long before David moved in with Samantha, a stranger had offered to meet with him early one morning to discuss David's latest brilliant scheme. Confident that his luck had changed, David indulged in an anticipatory drinking celebration the night before and then slept through the morning. "Why didn't you wake me?" he had yelled at his wife.

The timid girl knelt before him, trembling with fear at his rage, but David didn't care. "I tried to," she stammered. "But you wouldn't wake up. Last night, you . . . you drank too much."

"You're not blaming this on me, woman." The words were as hard and cold as David's eyes. In anger, he walked out the door and never returned. After all, why should he take care of someone who couldn't even be depended upon to wake him up?

The stranger wasn't interested in David's excuses, and another big plan for instant riches disappeared into the desert dust. All because of a woman. Why couldn't he find someone who could help him out for once? Why did he always have to be the one to take care of things?

David wandered around, remaining aloof from the others as the auction continued. Finally, it was his turn, but by then most of the crowd was gone. David placed a minimum reserve of five copper coins for the cow.

The auctioneer cleared his throat and said, "Attention, please. We now offer lot number eighty-one. This is a fine milk cow and will be a bargain for any buyer." The same tousled stock boy paraded the cow in front of the few remaining bidders. "The starting bid for this prize beast is a mere five pieces of copper," said the auctioneer glibly.

David rubbed his hands together, ignoring the hisses of disdain from the few remaining buyers. All he could

Chapter Four

think about was the money he would soon have in his purse. He patted the spot where the coins would lay hidden beneath his sash.

The auctioneer continued his spiel. "Let me have five. Do I hear five pieces for this fine animal? Look at that hide. Beautiful markings, aren't they? And the richest milk this side of the Jordan River."

The bidders murmured among themselves. Some began to walk away, and no one lifted a hand to place a bid.

The auctioneer motioned to David. "Better drop your price or you'll be walking this one home," he whispered.

David fumed. "No less than four," he finally agreed.

The auctioneer shouted toward the remaining men. "Gentlemen, I have exciting news. The cow can be yours for only four pieces of copper. Who will bid four? Who will be the first to take advantage of this magnanimous offer?"

One man stepped forward. "Three pieces. Take it or leave it."

With a broad smile, the auctioneer acknowledged the man's bid. "Three pieces. I have three pieces. Now do I hear four? Anybody? Don't let this marvelous beast go for such a bargain."

As the few remaining men grew restless, the auctioneer turned again to David. "It's the best you're going to get."

David looked at the crowd, his eyes smoldering, then jerked his head at the auctioneer. Quickly, the man announced, "Sold!"

The winning bidder stepped forward to take the halter.

"You stole this one," David said hotly.

The cow's new owner laughed. "Sure, I did."

David walked toward the clerk, kicking up dust in front of him. When he got to the table, he slammed his fist on it. "Let's get this done. I've got things to do and places to be."

The clerk sat back. "I'm sorry the crowd didn't hold out," he said, his voice dripping with insincerity. "We had a record attendance this morning. So many people . . ."

"Just give me my money," David interrupted. "This is just another scam."

The cashier counted out the three coins. David knocked the man's ledger to the ground as he snatched up the copper coins. "Oh, did I do that?" he said, sneering. He kicked dirt onto the pages before turning on his heel. "Don't worry. You won't see me here again." David walked away, oblivious to the stares of the men who watched him go.

Three coins. And nowhere to go. When he was out of sight of the stockyards, he stopped in the middle of the road to place the three precious coins in his pouch. Now what? He wasn't ready to face Samantha.

Standing beneath the steaming sun, David felt as small and insignificant as the price he had won for the cow.

He felt empty. Like the desert wilderness he had trekked through that morning.

He felt lost, standing on a dusty road with nowhere to go.

Chapter Five

SAMANTHA HAD WALKED only a few hundred yards in the direction of Jacob's well when she noticed a tiny silhouette on the horizon. She squinted against the harsh sun as she stared at the horizon of the distant landscape. As the distance between Samantha and the silhouette decreased, she recognized Tambia, the village soothsayer. At least it was Tambia's claim that she could foretell the gender of an unborn child and predict impending heartache or death. But Samantha wasn't fooled by Tambia's boasting. She knew the old woman had a gift for adding gossip to facial expressions that others overlooked. Tambia's words always left wounds.

In desert villages such as the one that birthed Samantha and Tambia, little changed from one decade to the next. Like their long-gone ancestors, the villagers thrived on the juicy details and tragic experiences of their neighbors. The misfortune of others seemed to provide a soothing balm of self-righteousness to those who most relished the sharing of gossip. And Tambia had the well-earned reputation of being the biggest gossip in the entire region of Samaria.

The stony path provided no way to avoid the shrunken woman. Samantha gave a slight nod without slowing her pace.

"Did you hear that whore Pazia was caught in the act?" Tambia's voice, guttural and loud as compensation for her deafness, scraped through the quiet morning heat.

At the news, Samantha stopped. *Not Pazia.* Samantha had not thought of her younger sister in ages. But she wouldn't let Tambia see any signs that the announcement disturbed her.

"What act?" Samantha asked, an innocent smile pasted on her face.

"You know what act." Tambia harrumphed and stammered. "Of all the women in Samaria, you certainly know what act."

Samantha felt her face redden, but she mustered what dignity she could and stood as straight as possible. "How do you know this?"

"I hear things, I do." Tambia lowered her voice to a conspiratorial whisper. "They caught her in the act, and you know what that means."

Despite the day's heat, Samantha shuddered. Without waiting for a response, Tambia continued. "They'll stone her, you know. It's the law."

"What about the man?"

"What about him? It's only the women who are punished in this life."

Chapter Five

Samantha nodded a silent assent.

Tambia's eyes flickered, just for a brief moment, with compassion. "Those Jews think they are so holy. The chosen ones. Hmph! We are only dogs to them."

Samantha turned, and as she walked away, she heard Tambia shouting after her. "People need to watch how they live. They need to make sure they get in the right bed at night."

It took every ounce of Samantha's willpower to keep her jar balanced on her shoulder instead of hurling it at the hateful old woman. Her stomach hurt as she thought of the news that Tambia had brought back with her from the south.

Poor Pazia. The girl was much younger than Samantha, and they didn't share the same father. Her mother had seldom spoken of Pazia after she ran off to Jerusalem with a young traveler who had set up camp on the plains between Sychar and Shechem. But once in a while, like today, some tidbit of news would travel from that holy city of Jerusalem even to the outcast plains of Samaria.

Samantha knew she should feel something profound. After all, her baby sister was probably dead. But she only felt numb, as if one of the heavy rocks used for the executions by stoning pressed on a heart already dead from an excess of sorrow and abuse. All she could do was say a prayer for the girl. Perhaps death was better for women like her mother and Pazia than the lives they were forced to live. The life she was forced to live.

Lost in her thoughts, Samantha didn't notice the group of men coming toward her on the path until they were only a short distance away. They were quiet, and though they were still too far away for Samantha to read their expressions, she knew they were watching her with cautious eyes. Gripping the water pitcher with one hand, she adjusted her shawl with her free hand so it covered the bottom half of her face.

So many of them. Samantha did a quick count, a task made more difficult because they began to walk closer to each other as the distance lessened. She counted again. Yes, there were twelve. And Jews by their look. What could they possibly be doing here in Samaria? And so close to Sychar?

Without a thought, Samantha stepped from the path and walked toward an untidy pile of rocks that embellished the desert plain. She positioned herself so she could keep an eye on the travelers without making it obvious that she was looking at them. As the men walked by her, they glanced her way. Quick, sharp looks meant to show their superiority, both in gender and heritage.

Ptui! Samantha spat as the last one passed by and stared at their receding backs. Not one turned around, but now she could hear the murmur of voices. So they had waited till they were beyond her before speaking to each other. Who cared? She waited a couple more minutes, then returned to the path to continue her dusty trek to the well.

Jews! Always they held their heads so high. Samantha knew that many of the Jewish people refused to step even one foot inside the boundaries of Samaria. On their trips from Jerusalem, south of Samaria, to the northern Galilean regions, many Jewish travelers headed east and crossed the Jordan River. Then they traveled north to the

Chapter Five

Dead Sea region. Only then would they head west and cross the Jordan River again. All that time and trouble just to keep from contaminating their precious sandals with Samaritan dirt.

The enmity between the Samaritans and the Judeans stretched back centuries to the days when the Assyrian Empire had destroyed the northern kingdom of Israel. The few Hebrews who remained in the region married other settlers, not of the Jewish faith. The Samaritan people came from these unions and households. Samantha didn't know when the capital city of Samaria was built, but she had heard the talk of village elders. In long memory, a quiet war persisted between the city of Samaria and the city of Jerusalem for power and strength.

As Samantha approached the well, thoughts of Pazia and the Jewish strangers were all wrapped up with each other. Had men like these travelers killed her sister? Did one of them throw a rock onto her broken body in punishment for the girl's wickedness? And what of her own life? If they had known her circumstances, would they have pelted her with the pebbles strewn along the dusty road? Better to die in the desert than by an executioner's cruel hands. Perhaps that was what she should do. Continue on, out onto the wilderness plain, until she could walk no farther. Then lie down and wait for death to come.

She could see the well now. Her thirst returned, and Samantha couldn't help but anticipate the feel of the cool water on her warm face. Then she saw him. A man sitting beside the well. With a start, she looked around. No companions. No cattle or sheep. Who could he be? Another stranger and no doubt a Jew. Just as well. He wouldn't speak to her. What self-respecting Jew ever spoke to a Samaritan? And certainly not a Samaritan woman! She was certain he, like the other men, would avoid any contact with her.

The thought occurred to her that he was a companion of the other travelers. But that was no concern of hers except that it would have been better if he had joined them on the path to Sychar. Then she could have drawn her water without his bothersome presence.

She slowed her steps, hoping he would go on his way. At first she felt nervous about approaching the well with the stranger so near to it. But as he watched her come closer and made no effort to move away, she became angry. The hot sun was now scorching and she could feel the perspiration on her arms and legs. She was drained, both physically and emotionally. And she was thirsty. She wanted a long drink of the cool, clear water. The directness of his gaze upon her both irritated and frightened her.

Approaching the well, she set her tall pitcher on the rim. *Get the water and go*, she told herself. *Get it and go.*

He spoke and Samantha jumped. "Give me a drink."

Chapter Six

DAVID STOOD ON the dirt path, gathering his thoughts and sorting out his plans for the rest of the day. The growling that began deep in his stomach helped clarify his priorities. He was hungry. Instead of going back to the dim hut and Samantha, he would go farther south to Shechem. There he could get food. Maybe even some wine. And why shouldn't he? He was the one who got up at the crack of dawn to walk Samantha's crazy cow to the auction stockyards. If he turned all three coins over to Samantha, he might not get any use from them at all. Definitely, he needed to go to Shechem and enjoy a good meal. His mood brightened by the decision, David headed off across the countryside, avoiding the worn path back to Sychar altogether.

For as long as he could remember, David had been a wanderer. It was as if he were always on the lookout for the scenery he hadn't seen, the experience he hadn't experienced. Maybe it was an innate sense of adventure. Or perhaps it was some unrecognized need to avoid the dull ache that accompanied his existence.

This drive for change littered David's past with pitfalls and boulders. First, it was moving from one place to another. Then it was jobs. Changing careers, dreaming big dreams of quick wealth. And the women. Married twice and now living with a woman he didn't love in a rundown hut that didn't belong to him.

Of course, he wasn't to blame for any of his troubles. His intentions were always honorable, always the best. He couldn't help it if other people didn't see things the same way he did. How could he be held responsible for the problems of others?

As he walked along, David's thoughts were as scattered as the tiny dust clouds that stirred at his feet. He thought about his first wife and the early days of their courtship. Certainly, he believed they would always be together. But after only a short time her sweet disposition became a grating irritant. Who could fault him for finding comfort with someone who laughed at his stories instead of berating him to make something of himself? And then, there had been the incident with the fig tree. How ridiculous was that?

With his dark wavy hair, deep brown eyes, and strong good looks, David never lacked attention for long. Not before, between, or after his marriages. Attractive women could always be found to attend his needs. How often in his youth had he bragged to his friends that he had never been a day without a woman. Thinking of that boast today, beneath the steamy desert sun, David felt a chill in

Chapter Six

his heart. He stopped walking without even realizing it. "Never a day without a woman," he whispered to himself. "But alone all my life."

The intense heat bore down on the solitary man, draining him of strength. His fine linen tunic, a leftover from days of prosperity, felt damp from his sweat, and his mind weighed heavy with truths too powerful to bear. For a fleeting moment, he wondered if God was punishing him for the decisions he had made in the past. But long years of ignoring such quiet nudges pushed this one aside before it could take root in the thorny ground of David's heart.

"My day is coming," he shouted to the blue sky. "One day I'll be rich! I'll show them all!"

With riches would come the right woman. The perfect wife to share his life—the one who could keep him happy forever. David whistled a jaunty little tune as he continued the journey into Shechem.

No one was around to watch David walk purposefully across the countryside or hear his joyful whistle. If someone had been there, that person might have felt a pang of jealousy toward a traveler who seemed so contented with life and his place in it. But they would have been deceived. For in the depths of David's heart, he knew he had a need that could never be filled by riches.

Chapter Seven

"GIVE ME A drink." The man's voice resonated with assurance and an indefinable quality that seemed to worm its way into Samantha's bitter heart. Samantha stood, silent as a stone statue, as the stranger's words enveloped her. She wanted to run, but her feet refused to move. She raised her head slowly and found herself drawn into the warm gaze of the stranger. He was a Jew. And yet he was asking her, a Samaritan woman, for a drink from Jacob's well. Samantha's astonishment finally found voice.

"How is it that you're a Jew and me a Samaritan and you ask me for a drink?" Her voice sounded high, unnatural. The stranger didn't reply and Samantha cleared her throat, all the while clutching the water jar with both hands. She consciously relaxed her grip, stretching her fingers. "Why are you in my country? Do you think I

Chapter Seven

don't know that Jewish travelers avoid us? They treat us and our land as though we are a plague."

The stranger continued looking at her, but not in a way that any man had ever looked at Samantha before. She was used to the raucous leers of drunken men, the silent appraisal from the villagers when their wives weren't looking. She had seen pity mixed with distaste in the glances of the temple priests. But never a look like this. The stranger's eyes penetrated into her very soul, frightening her and reassuring her at the same time. She could not even pretend to be insulted that he spoke to her or to assume that his intentions were dishonorable.

"If you knew the gift of God and who was asking," he said, his voice low and smooth, "you would be asking me for a drink."

Samantha took in the words, repeating them silently to herself. *Asking him for a drink?* She shook her head. *He's not making any sense.* And yet, there was something about him that kept her rooted to that one spot. If any other man had suggested such a thing, she would have laughed in his face. But there was nothing crazy about this man.

"How could you do that?" she finally asked. "You don't have a bucket and this well is very deep." At least her voice was no longer squeaking. That gave her confidence. "Are you greater than our father Jacob who dug this well?"

The stranger's mouth curved into a small smile and Samantha found herself smiling back. What power he had over her, she could not imagine. His dark hair curled over a broad forehead and his cheekbones appeared gaunt with weariness. No one would call him handsome, and yet Samantha found herself thinking she had never met anyone more beautiful. She blushed at the thought.

"If you drink this," the stranger said, gesturing at the well's opening, "you'll be thirsty again tomorrow. But if you ever take a drink of my water, you'll never thirst again. What I give will be a well springing into everlasting life."

Aching joy and exquisite hurt squeezed Samantha's spirit as the stranger's simple words washed over her. She had no wisdom to describe what she was experiencing, though suddenly she was reminded of the birth of her son. The squeezing, horrendous, tearing pains of childbirth woven together with the reckless joy of cradling the mewling infant in her arms. This was the same, and yet so different.

Without thinking about what she was doing, Samantha threw herself at the stranger's feet. Hitting the hot ground with the palm of her hand, she pleaded, "Sir, I want this water. I don't want to be thirsty anymore and I don't want to stay in this place."

"Go get your husband."

Samantha dared not raise her head. How could she look into those warm, piercing eyes and admit her sin? "I have no husband," she said, her voice barely above a whisper. And then her heart broke. Tears flowed over the soft contours of her bronzed cheeks.

With the rough fingers of a stonemason, the stranger lifted her chin and looked again into Samantha's eyes. "It's true you have no husband, though you have had five. Yet the man you live with now is not your husband."

Chapter Seven

Samantha sat backward on her heels, totally lost in the deep caverns of her past, as she stared at the stranger in amazement. *He said five. How could he possibly have known?* Images appeared before her, so vivid and real that she thought she could touch them. She stretched her arms to the empty air. Yes, there had been five. Each one, in his own way, hurting her worse than the one before. But Titus, her second. No one knew about him. Not even nosy Tambia.

How? Samantha screamed silently, then scooted quickly back, away from the stranger, in fear and despair. *How did this Jewish stranger know?*

Chapter Eight

FINALLY ARRIVING AT the outskirts of the bustling town, David thought how much he hated Samaria. Something in the very air seemed to smother every dream he ever had. As he passed first one house and then another, memories rose before him like dusty mirages. Hunger had driven him in this direction, but perhaps it had been a mistake to follow that impulse. The fourth house was identical to the others, though perhaps a little smaller. This was the hut where David had lived with his first wife.

He stopped before the small courtyard, shaded by a large, multi-trunked fig tree, in front of the house. David remembered the difficulties he had planting the tree, but he hadn't minded the trouble. All the time he was watering and tending the young seedling, he thought about the fruit it would someday bear. But with each

Chapter Eight

passing season, the tree proved barren. David became irrational with frustration.

There was the day that David's mother-in-law brought him a fig pie, fresh from her stone oven. It smelled sweet and warm. David's mouth watered in anticipation of taking that first large bite. But when he finished the delicious treat, his satisfaction turned to irritation. He could see his own fig tree, growing but still barren, through his open door. The tree's failure to bear figs seemed a deliberate insult, and David had just about lost his patience.

After a morning quarrel with his young wife over some now-forgotten grievance, David stormed out of the house. As he rushed to the road, a low-hanging branch from the tree scratched his face, coming dangerously close to his eye.

"I hate you," David yelled at the tree. His wife came to the doorway to see what was wrong and David turned to her. "I hate you," he shouted again. He left the courtyard, but soon returned with an axe.

"No," screamed his young wife. Before David realized what she was doing, the distraught girl threw her arms around the tree. "Please don't cut it down," she begged, tears streaming down her face. "Please don't cut it down."

Though David was stunned by his wife's reaction, he couldn't let her know that. "Why not?" he demanded. "It's produced absolutely no fruit. And look what happened to me."

"One more year," his wife sobbed. "Just one. If it doesn't bear fruit next harvest, then you can cut it down and throw it into the fire. Just one more year."

David threw the axe at his wife's feet. "Agreed." His harsh voice grated in the air between them. "If it bears no fruit next year, *you* will cut it down!"

But David wasn't there at the next season to know whether the tree bore fruit. Now, as he stood beneath its shade and remembered all the quarrels, he realized that the flourishing tree had stretched its roots deep into the soil, like giant fingers gripping the ground. "I wonder if I would have grown roots if I had stayed here," he murmured. He turned his attention to the house. The wooden fence was rotting, and the post where he used to tie his prize donkey was rubbed smooth with use. Though everything else looked old and used up, the tree spread its limbs to the sun and seemed to reign over the entire yard.

David recalled his father telling him once that every living thing was always growing. Even people. "They may stop growing up, but they keep on growing old. If you ever stop growing, David, it's because you're dead." Those long-ago words of his father drew David further into memory. He was a young boy again, sitting beside his father as they fished for supper. "What day did the grass grow, son?" his father asked. David gave his father a quizzical look. He didn't know how to answer the strange question. When he didn't reply, his father asked another question. "What day did your feet grow, son?"

David peered at his bare toes, half-hidden in the tall grass beside the pond. His father laughed, warm and hearty. "Well, David, you needed new shoes this year. Your feet are bigger than they were last year. What day did they grow?"

Chapter Eight

"I don't know, Father."

"They are always growing." The older man mussed his son's curly locks. "Important things like grass and boys grow so slowly, you can't see it happening. But you know when it has happened by the end result."

Standing by the large fig tree, David shook his head to clear it of his father's words. Then he looked again into the upper branches of the tree. "You never stopped growing," he whispered. "But I did."

The door to the house opened and David wiped his misty eyes with the back of his hand. A small boy darted out, spied David, and ran back into the house before David could even say *shalom*.

David pulled a fat fig from a low-hanging branch and thought again of his father and that day at the pond. He couldn't have been much older than the young boy living in that house now. Suddenly David felt tired. He missed being a boy and he missed the talks he and his father used to have. But it was too late for missing now. His father was far away, and David could never be a boy again. David took a bite of the sweet fig. It tasted good in his dry mouth, but he also felt the taint of knowing he would never eat from that tree again.

Life, David thought. *It's full of "could haves" and "should haves" But only madness awaits a man who lives in the world of "what if."* Shaking his head, he followed the main road into the center of town and its busy marketplace.

Chapter Nine

SAMANTHA HAD MET Titus during her one and only trip to the western borders of Samaria. Her uncle, a potter, took her and one of her brothers to the bustling seaport of Caesarea to help him with a new business venture. Only a few months before, Samantha had been abandoned by her first husband, a childhood sweetheart who promised her the moon but gave her nothing but stardust.

She didn't want to go with her uncle Jonas. She didn't want to do anything but sit in the garden behind her mother's house. Here, among the patches of vegetables and herbs, she hid from the clucking tongues of the village hens. But her mother, wearied of Samantha's dark moods, gave her no choice. "Go with your uncle or go to the mountain temple," her mother said. "But get out of my sight."

Chapter Nine

On the first day in her uncle's new business, Titus swaggered in on some pretext of needing a new oil lamp. But later he confessed that he had seen Samantha enter the shop and wanted to get another glimpse of her dark beauty.

When Titus came through the door, Samantha felt her breath catch in her throat at the sight of the broad Roman soldier. His chestnut hair, underneath a decorated helmet, framed a chiseled face, his features as distinctive as one of the heathen gods caught in marble and displayed in the town center. Massive arms and legs were encased in brilliantly polished armor that captured and held even the tiniest rays of light. His green-flecked eyes twinkled with a merriment that seemed to well up from some place deep within him. Samantha had never seen anyone with such light eyes, and she was fascinated by the way they seemed to lighten and darken depending on Titus's mood. For his part, Titus was enthralled with Samantha's tall, slender grace and fine features.

Samantha's uncle raged against the Roman soldiers who patrolled the Caesarean streets, but only when they weren't around, of course. Too many soldiers for comfort seemed to prefer Jonas's bowls and cups than those of the other potters. Jonas appreciated the business. After all, Roman coins were as valuable as any other. But he distrusted the too-proud warriors who swaggered around town like a conquering army. Of course, that's what they were, but Jonas didn't like the constant reminder.

From the little nook where she performed her household chores, Samantha agreed with her uncle's rantings and ravings. But when Titus stopped by the shop a third and then a fourth time, her eyes sent a wordless message to the handsome soldier. Only a few days later, Titus managed to block her path when she was in the marketplace on one of her uncle's errands. Less than a week later, Samantha had become quite skilled at sneaking from her room at night. And she always managed to make it back home before anyone knew she was gone.

Titus was amused at the bravado of his "little Samaritan swallow." Samantha pretended to despise the pet name, but her heart jumped every time he whispered it into her ear. He taught her to drink the strong water-laced rum and encouraged her to dance for him and his companions.

Samantha was aware that his friends wanted her and that Titus enjoyed their longing. All they could do was watch in jealous adoration. Titus laughed at Samantha's discomfort in performing for them. As Samantha gracefully twirled and swayed in time to the music's pulsing rhythm, Titus watched her closely. And when Samantha collapsed breathlessly into his arms at the dance's end, he kissed her soundly. "Again, my love," he said. She saw him looking around at his pals, noting the lecherous gleams in their drunken eyes. "Dance again." His hearty laughter erupted from his chest.

Samantha despised the lechery, but she adored Titus. The handsome Roman cast a spell over her so that any good judgment she had flew away, leaving her heart open to his pleasure. "Please," he said, though Samantha knew the word was only a courtesy. Titus would never beg for anything he wanted. It didn't matter. Ignoring her hesitations, she got up and danced once more, keeping

Chapter Nine

her eyes only on Titus and imagining that he was the only one watching her.

A short week later, Titus proposed and they married in a secret ceremony amid a copse of olive trees. Titus took her to a private room for their wedding night, but before the sun broke over the horizon, he sent her back to her uncle's home. "Tell no one of our marriage, my little swallow," he whispered between kisses. "Let it be our secret awhile longer."

"But why?" Samantha asked, feeling the tendrils of fear crawling around her heart.

"I have my reasons." Titus kissed her again, then got up and began dressing. "But come back tonight. I'll be waiting."

Throughout the following days, Samantha spent her working hours confused and distracted. Only her fear that her uncle would discover her secret helped keep her mind on her tasks. Each evening as she left Jonas's house, she resolved to tell Titus that he must tell her uncle about their wedding. That he must provide a home for her.

But as soon as she entered Titus's private room, he swirled her around in his arms and kissed away all her words and fears. Samantha fell asleep in his comforting embrace, and her doubts left her alone until morning.

One afternoon, Samantha returned from an errand to find Jonas in deep conversation with another man. She recognized him as a competitor who kept a shop on a nearby street. When the man left, Jonas called Samantha into the back room. "I've sold the shop," he said. "We'll be returning to Sychar within the month."

Samantha's stomach dropped and a roaring began in her ears. Had she heard him right? Certainly he couldn't mean it. He couldn't take her away.

"Why?"

Her uncle glared at her. "Who are you to question my decisions? We have packing and cleaning to do. Get busy."

That night, Samantha fell into Titus's arms, tears streaming down her face. When he kissed her, she turned her face away and stepped back. "My uncle is leaving. He said I had to go with him."

Titus looked at her, but his eyes were dark and Samantha had no idea what he was thinking. "When?"

"Less than a month."

"Hmm." Titus shrugged his powerful shoulders in a playful gesture. "That doesn't give us much time, does it?" He drew Samantha back into his arms, but she resisted his pull.

"You're going to let me go?" She choked back a sob. "Why did you marry me if you didn't want me with you?"

"I want you with me very much. Surely I've proved that," he said with a grin. When Samantha didn't respond, he grew serious. "My legion leaves in the morning. We go to the coasts of Africa to wage a campaign. When I return, I will talk to your uncle."

"When you return? When will that be?"

"Ten days. Two weeks at the most." Titus reached for Samantha's hand. "We only have to show our strength. The battle has already been won."

Chapter Nine

In the wee morning hours, Samantha woke to the sounds of Titus moving about the room. "You're leaving," she said.

Titus picked up his sword. "When you hear of our return, go to the olive grove. We will meet there."

"Yes. I will be there." As he closed the door, she repeated the words. "I will be there."

Through the following days, Samantha alternated between worrying about Titus and dreaming of a future with him. She imagined the two of them establishing a home in the exciting seaport city. Raising children along the shores of the Mediterranean Sea. A new life was beginning for her, an exciting life far from the desert wilderness of Samaria. Her uncle's daily rants and imperious orders fell on deaf ears as Samantha worked hard only to make the hours go more swiftly until the return of Titus and his army.

The tenth day came without the return of the Roman legion. Then the eleventh and the twelfth. Samantha listened eagerly for the first peals of the bells announcing the army's victorious return. She wanted to see the runner proclaiming the news throughout the streets: "Nike! Nike! Victory! Victory!" She knew that a festival would follow in the runner's footsteps. Banquets, drink, music. A crowd cheering the heroic soldiers as they came off the ship bearing the spoils of war.

Then she would go to the olive grove and wait for her Roman hero. Her husband. In between running errands for her uncle and tending to the household, she dreamed of what she would wear. In the late evenings, she stitched a bright embroidered pattern on a new linen tunic. The lush purple and gold threads enhanced the sheen of her bronze skin. She could already see the look of approval in Titus's clear, light eyes.

Another day passed and Samantha squelched her increasing worry with hard work.

On the fifteenth day, Jonas sent Samantha on an errand near the port. She was glad to leave the shop and her uncle's ominous glare. In the past few days, her spirits had drooped as each hour passed without the pealing of the bell or the runner's victorious cries.

When Samantha reached the large harbor port, she was surprised by the crowd gathered there. Recognizing an old woman who often came into her uncle's store, Samantha asked, "Why are all these people here?"

"Go home, child," the woman answered.

"Please tell me," Samantha insisted. "What is happening?"

The old woman sighed heavily. "We wait for the soldiers."

"They've arrived?" Samantha was incredulous. "But I heard no bells. No runner."

"The ship came in this morning. There was no need for bells and runners."

As the old woman's words penetrated Samantha's heart, her eyes widened. "No," she said, shaking her head. "No."

Then she turned away from the woman and ran into the crowd. Inch by terrible inch, she squeezed through the mass of humanity until she was at the waterfront. Against the backdrop of an endless dark sea and an amber sun, shrouded figures lay on the pier. The bodies of the

Chapter Nine

defeated dead. Samantha collapsed to the limestone street, her eyes intent on the few soldiers milling around the docks. But Titus never appeared.

In the fading rays of the setting sun, a soldier bent down and touched Samantha's shoulder. She recognized him as one of the men who watched her dance.

"Don't tell me," she said, her voice barely above a whisper.

The soldier raised her up by her elbows until she was standing. "Would you like me to escort you home?"

Samantha shook her head. Adjusting her veil on top of her head, she turned away from the soldier and walked back to the market center. With each step, she buried her grief deeper into her heart.

No one knew of her marriage to the Roman soldier. She had no ring, no evidence to prove it had ever taken place. All she had was a stone heart that threatened to burst her ribs with its weight. She resolved never to wait on a man again. They never came home.

Chapter Ten

AS DAVID REACHED the town center, he felt his spirits rise. He loved the hustle and bustle of city life. The crowded streets, teeming with activity, and all the selling and buying of the marketplace energized him. Even his tired feet seemed to feel renewed by the pulsing of the city's rhythm. He wandered past several stalls and shops, then saw exactly what he wanted. The sun marked the time as high noon and David's stomach agreed. The early-morning dates and the sweet fig had given only momentary nourishment and he was hungry.

The roadside merchant offered bread and wine for a small price and David had three coins in his pouch. He laughed. Suddenly he felt as wealthy as a king. It no longer mattered that the money technically belonged to Samantha. She couldn't expect him to take the cow to auction and come back again without something to eat. If she didn't want him spending money on food, she should

Chapter Ten

have got up before he did and made him something to take with him. It was her fault that he was hungry now.

The roadside café was little more than a hut with a small fire pit and oven, but in David's eyes, it looked as inviting as a banquet hall. Some men sat on the bench drawn up to the only table and others perched on two old tree stumps. But David didn't care. All the gloom of the morning's memories was swept away with the knowledge that he could afford a meal.

When the merchant approached, David smiled broadly. "Bread and wine, my friend," he said, a little too loudly. "I just sold a broken-down cow for much more than she was worth and now I'm hungry."

The other men perked up at the announcement, and a couple exchanged glances. They watched as David pulled the three copper coins from his pouch. Deliberately, peering from beneath his brows to make sure the others were watching, David placed one of the coins in the merchant's outstretched palm.

"This man needs wine," the merchant shouted to a young boy loitering in the shade. Then he shooed away those at the table. "Make room," he said, arms flapping. "Make room." He gestured to David to sit down as he wiped away the crumbs left by the previous patrons.

David swaggered to the table and sat down, self-importance glowing in his eyes. The owner poured purple wine into a wooden goblet, all the while apologizing that he didn't have a fancier cup for so worthy a gentleman. David made a big ceremony out of taking the first sip, knowing the merchant was eager for his approval. Well, he could be as magnanimous as anyone. He set the cup down with a flourish. "Best wine I've had all day," he said, mirth evident in his voice.

"Thank you, sir." The merchant bowed. He refilled David's cup, then hurried to get bread and fruit for his customer.

David glanced over at the patrons who had been shooed away from the table. They sat under the tree now, sullen looks on their faces that made David feel uncomfortable. He remembered a time when he was an invited guest to a banquet being held in honor of a very important man. David had strutted into the banquet hall, anxious for others to see him in his fine robes and colorful headdress. Noticing a seat at the front of the room, David's spirits had soared. Keeping an eye on it, hoping no one else would get to it before he did, David made his way to the coveted spot. He reclined on the couch and greeted his neighbor, who gave him a strange look. David dismissed it as jealousy.

Only a few moments passed, however, before a harried steward knelt before David, mumbling apologies and excuses. The couch was reserved for the important man's father. David would have to move. By now, all but the lesser seats in the back had been taken by other guests. David, embarrassed and fuming, stormed out of the banquet hall. Those who watched the little scene unfold only shook their heads. They had seen it before, times when David tried to lord it over others. Would he never learn?

David shook his head to clear it of the stale memory. Today others had to make room for him, and that's the way it should always be. He had money, good wine, and the envy of the other patrons. Too bad Samantha couldn't see him now.

Chapter Ten

Taking another sip of the refreshing wine, David thought back to his first wedding reception. The bride, though barely old enough for marriage, was a lovely girl of grace and delicacy. Even better, from David's viewpoint, her father was an extremely wealthy man who doted on his only daughter. David convinced her of his love and that she couldn't live without him as her husband. She convinced her father of the same thing.

Though usually a shrewd businessman, the man was blind when it came to the desires of his precious daughter. In truth, he had legitimate reservations about David's character. But marriage often settles a man. David agreed with this observation, so the bride's father generously forgave the hefty debts the younger man owed him. The father even paid David's other obligations.

David never stayed in good graces very long. One day the older man called David into his presence. "My steward tells me," the father-in-law said, "that you are owed a debt."

"That is true," David replied, obviously bored with the conversation.

"The debt is a large one?"

"Yes." David disclosed the amount.

The father-in-law's eyes widened. "David," he cried. "Think of your own debts that I paid on your behalf. This debt that is owed to you is but a gnat compared to a camel."

"May I leave now? Your daughter waits for me." David's words were polite, but his tone was as cold as the winter snows.

"I am told the man is now in prison."

"He is." David stood, his face an impassive mask over a growing rage. "And there he will stay."

The father-in-law's goodwill was lost that day. And the girl had not forgotten David's threats about the fig tree. At her father's urging and already stripped of her girlish delusions, David's wife finally gave up and returned to her father's welcoming arms. The man handled all the legal aspects of the divorce as quietly and efficiently as possible. David's easy life was torn out from under him before he even realized anything was happening.

The memories of his first wedding and the sweet taste of the merchant's new wine reminded David of a wedding reception he attended a year or so before in Cana. He and his friends drank as much of the free-flowing wine as they could until there was no more. The bride's father was distraught with embarrassment. But then it seemed he had gotten upset over nothing. More wine appeared and it was the best wine David had ever tasted. One of his friends had commented how strange it was that the bride's father hadn't served such good wine at the beginning of the reception instead of waiting till the end.

Then another friend pointed to a guest standing apart from the crowd. "He did it," the friend said. "He changed well water into wine."

David and the others laughed. But after that day, David often paused before taking a drink of water. *Someone please turn this water into wine.* Sitting at the roadside café, David thought again of the strange wedding guest. *Where is he now?* David wondered as he took another sip of his wine.

Chapter Eleven

Samantha returned to Sychar and her mother's poor hut. Though the embarrassment of her first marriage had kept her hidden in the garden, the secret of her second kept her hidden within herself. Her eyes lost what sparkle still remained and her mouth clinched in a perpetual straight line, neither smile nor frown. She did her chores and tasks, more even than before she left, but took no pleasure in them. She limited her movements and gestures to only those necessary to do what needed to be done and nothing more.

Her mother quizzed Jonas about the change, demanding to know what he had done with her daughter while she was under his care. But Jonas grew angry at her accusations and could give her no answers. He knew nothing except that Samantha had stayed out late one day and returned to the shop in this wooden state. She refused to tell him where she had been despite his threat of a good thrashing.

The promised thrashing never came. Samantha had worked harder than ever after that day, doing everything he asked of her and more. Because of Samantha's efforts, they left Caesarea earlier than planned and with less cost to his purse than anticipated. Jonas set a small pile of coins on the table in Samantha's hut, perhaps more than he originally intended. The next morning, he left with his potter's tools for Jerusalem.

Soon after arriving home, Samantha awoke to a certainty that she felt deep within. Her grief crystallized into fear. No one would believe the story of her marriage to a dead Roman soldier. How could she possibly explain the existence of the life she knew without any doubt was growing within her? Night after night she wrestled with her dilemma, each time reaching only one horrible solution. She needed a husband. And soon.

On the hot windless nights, Samantha often slept on the roof of the small flat-topped house. Lying on a thin woven mat, she looked up into the heavens at the night's constellations and thought about Titus. She loved him, but she knew nothing about him. Nothing about his family or even how he died. In her most honest moments, Samantha could see that her marriage had fulfilled one need only. But what else mattered when one was being kissed and held by a man so strong, so handsome? Instead of healing with the salve of time, Samantha became more convinced of Titus's perfections. He had no flaws she could identify, and her grief compounded with that knowledge.

Chapter Eleven

Lying below the stars, she thought of the eligible men of her village and compared each one to the perfect standard of the Roman soldier who filled her heart. Not one was worthy enough to be considered as the father of Titus's child. But as more days passed, Samantha knew that despite her qualms she could delay no longer.

For reasons Samantha could not fathom, her thoughts often drifted during this time to her first husband. Stephen and Samantha had known each other since they were children, playing with all the others in the village after the chores were done. No one seemed surprised when their parents arranged their betrothal. It was almost an anticlimactic announcement, since it seemed everyone had taken for granted that the two would someday marry.

During the betrothal time, a new family settled in the small village. They had a daughter, Litia, about Samantha's age, and the two girls quickly became friends and confidantes. Litia listened, and even cried, when Samantha told her about the endless, hopeless nights of waiting for her father's return. She rejoiced at Samantha's upcoming marriage to the handsome Stephen and helped in every possible way with the wedding arrangements.

At first it seemed natural to Samantha that her best friend would also be friends with her husband. But it wasn't long till Samantha began feeling the uneasiness of suspicion. She tried in vain to talk herself out of what everyone else in the village seemed to know.

Samantha realized that Litia appeared to know personal details about her marriage to Stephen. Petty arguments between the newlyweds became out-and-out battles as the months went by. And Litia appeared to be siding with Stephen when Samantha confided in her.

Then the unthinkable happened. Samantha knocked on Litia's door and Stephen's voice shouted to her. "Go home!"

The subsequent divorce branded Samantha as a scorned woman, and as sometimes happens, Stephen came through the scandal, not only with Litia, but also his reputation. In most cases Litia would have been stoned, but Stephen knew all the right people to make problems go away. After all, he had business interests, and the villagers couldn't afford to snub him, no matter how badly he treated Samantha.

How different my life would have been, Samantha thought, *if Litia had never come.* But such thoughts couldn't help her now. She had a problem and she needed a husband.

The upcoming festival provided the answer. Samantha bathed in the clear water of the nearby wadi and brushed her newly washed hair until it glistened as dark as a raven's blue-black feathers. She carefully dressed so that her still slender figure showed itself to advantage, both demure and inviting. She forced herself to smile, trying again and again until she felt the muscles around her eyes relax.

Villagers from several small towns attended the festival and Samantha met up with friends she hadn't seen in years. They gathered together, drinking wine and sharing news. One told the astonishing story of a twelve-year-old boy who attended the Passover in Jerusalem recently.

Chapter Eleven

"He astounded the temple priests with his knowledge." Another chimed in, "I heard that too. They say he knows all the Scriptures."

"Perhaps he is a prophet," said another.

Samantha took a bunch of grapes and popped one into her mouth. *In a couple of months, no one will need a prophet to know what I did this summer*, Samantha thought.

As the others continued talking about the young boy, Samantha scanned the crowd. Her attention was caught by a loud, obnoxious man standing at the wine counter. He slammed his hand on the counter just as another man bumped into him. Wine was spilled and the loud man punched the other in the face.

Someone screamed as fists began flying. The festival was now a bawling ruckus. Samantha and her group moved toward the back of the crowd out of harm's way. When the fighting ceased, they returned to their table.

Before Samantha could sit down, her chair was pulled away from the table. "Allow me," said a husky masculine voice. Samantha looked into the eyes of the obnoxious man who had started the fistfight. He wasn't much taller than she, but he was large-chested and powerfully built. Samantha thanked him and sat down. "My name is Barabbas."

"I am Samantha."

Barabbas sat down in a nearby chair, bringing it closer to Samantha. She could see that his dark hair was thinning, showing patches of a sunburned scalp. Samantha's stomach churned. But what difference did it really make? He was as good as any other. He smiled at her and Samantha smiled back. A few days later, they were married.

Samantha soon learned that Barabbas was not as good as any other. His scarred knuckles were proof of many battles, both won and lost. Those he couldn't intimidate with his angry scowls were intimidated by his beefy fists. Her baby would have a father, but at a horrible price.

CHAPTER TWELVE

AFTER INDULGING IN his wine and devouring the warm, oven-fresh bread, David leaned back in the chair. His stomach was no longer growling, he had money in his pouch, there was nowhere he had to be.

One of the other patrons caught his attention. "Are you from Jerusalem, stranger?"

David laughed. "No, I'm a simple farmer." He grinned at his own cleverness. It's what he always said when people asked about his occupation. But the truth was he hated farming and had spent as little time as he possibly could in fields and pastures. The only thing David liked about farming was the harvest—as long as someone else did the actual work. David enjoyed the fresh fruits and ripe vegetables. He loved to reap, but he sure didn't like to sow.

Still, farming was his heritage. David had grown up watching his father amass a sizeable fortune one harvest at a time. Every morning, as the family gathered around the breakfast table, his father joined hands with David's mother and blessed the food. "The word of the Lord declares those who sow sparingly shall reap sparingly," his father recited in his melodious tenor. "Those who sow bountifully shall reap bountifully. Let us get up from this table and use this day to sow good things for those we encounter along our way."

Because of his father's large land holdings, David had once been a rich man. With no intentions of being saddled with farming responsibilities, he insisted his father give him his inheritance and took off for big-city life. Yes, that's the life he should have been born into.

Still, thinking about his father now, David felt a sadness descend. He had left home ten years ago, and in that short time, he had spent his inheritance, married two women, and drunk more bottles of wine than most men consume in a lifetime. And now here he was, acting like some big shot at a roadside café because he had a couple of coins in his pocket. Coins that weren't even his.

David left the merchant's table and wandered the city streets, thinking of his father and the life he had left on the farm. When he was younger, David often felt his father kept him from having fun. After all, they had servants to take care of the land and the cattle. But his father always wanted David and his older brother to work, too. The old man was so demanding with his constant preaching and prayers. At one time, David thought he hated his father. But as he walked this dusty street so far from home, his heart ached to see the older man again.

Chapter Twelve

David turned a corner and practically stumbled over some men casting lots. His heart went from aching to pounding in less time than it took for him to reach for the purse at his waist. He was a pro at dice games, though it seemed he remembered the few times he won and forgot the many times he lost. No matter. The coins were in his hand and he was ready to play. After all, what were two paltry coins when riches could be made. Even Samantha would be impressed when he came home with a full pouch.

"Give me room, boys," David said as he crowded between the players. "I'm feeling lucky."

Chapter Thirteen

SAMANTHA AND BARABBAS were the talk of the town. They kept the night life in business, attending every party they heard about whether or not they were invited. Not one host had the courage or size to insist that Barabbas behave with decorum. Eventually Samantha's growing belly gave her the excuse to stay home from these wild nights. The town gossips made sure Samantha knew all about Barabbas's fistfights and philandering. Samantha pretended humiliation, but her heart rejoiced that her evenings were spent alone and in peace.

At the fish market, Samantha overheard the talk.

"You never know what that Barabbas will do next." The grizzled fisherman spat. "He might fight you or he might kiss you."

His companion laughed. "He can hit me or kiss me as long as he doesn't kill me."

Chapter Thirteen

Samantha shuddered and pulled her cloak more tightly around her pregnant body. The memory of the slap Barabbas had given her only two days before sent her head reeling again. What had she been thinking to marry such a brute? Surely the shame of an unwed pregnancy would have been easier to endure than the humiliation and heartache of being married to such a man.

As the weeks passed by, Samantha became more afraid of her husband's drunken bouts of anger. But even in the rare moments of his sobriety, Barabbas could terrorize her. "That child you're carrying," he said, gesturing one morning as he stuffed huge chunks of milk-soaked bread into his mouth. "You know it's a boy."

"I can't know that," Samantha replied, keeping her voice as quiet and level as possible.

"I'm just warning you." Barabbas poked his finger into her abdomen. "A girl-child is going in the river. So you better be sure it's a boy." He stood up and stretched, then headed for the door. "I need a strong boy to help out in the fields." With a laugh, he left, leaving Samantha to tremble with anger and disgust.

"Help in the field," she muttered to herself. All Barabbas ever did in the field was pick whatever he intended to eat for himself. She did all the hoeing and weeding and watering. He only showed up to reap the harvest. Other than that, he stayed with his group of thieves, stealing and plundering throughout Samaria.

Samantha thanked God that Barabbas was away the morning her water broke. A neighbor sent for Samantha's mother and the midwife. Throughout the hot morning, Samantha strained to birth the life in her womb. Through her pain, she stifled the flood of sadness and fear that threatened her. *Please be a boy*, she silently begged while she determined in her heart that a daughter would be sent home with her mother.

If Barabbas was joking, she would bring the girl home. If he was serious, she would make arrangements with her mother to raise the child. Samantha remembered the ancient story the elders told of the baby Moses. How Moses' mother fashioned an ark out of reeds and sealed it with slime and tar to keep it dry. As a little girl, Samantha loved that story. God protected the baby Moses from the dangers of the giant Nile River and placed him in the arms of Pharaoh's daughter. *Will God protect my baby?* Samantha groaned with the pain of another difficult contraction. *Can God turn my baby into a prince?*

The long day continued and Samantha noticed the worried glances being exchanged between her mother and the midwife.

"What is it?" Samantha's ragged voice sounded so weary.

Her mother brushed the damp hair from Samantha's eyes. "The baby is a large one."

The neighbor turned to the midwife and whispered, "I fear for her life."

Samantha heard the whisper and wept. Would she die without ever having lived? This child, Titus's child, was all she loved. Thinking of Titus, Samantha recalled the loneliness she felt on the wharf waiting for him to come off the ship. His gentle laugh reverberated in her brain. *No! Titus's child will live.*

Chapter Thirteen

Supported on the birthing stool by her mother and neighbor, Samantha gritted her teeth. The midwife applied her special herbs and ointments while directing Samantha's breathing. Samantha stifled the scream that threatened to expel the last bit of strength from her body. At the midwife's urging, she pushed her body through the rending, wrenching, tearing pain. And a new life, along with the cry that accompanies all struggles for freedom, came forth.

Tears drenched Samantha's cheeks as she reached for the naked infant.

"A boy," the midwife announced with pride as if she had something to do with the child's gender.

"A boy," Samantha whispered as she gently examined the little face, the tiny fingers and toes. *Thank you, O Lord. Thank you.*

The midwife took the infant from Samantha and performed her ministrations. Once the infant was washed and tightly swaddled, she returned him to Samantha, who held him to her breast for his first taste of nourishment.

A shadow filled the room. Barabbas. Samantha's mother fussed with the coverings and kept her back to the man. The midwife stared at him. "Thank God, sir. You have a son."

Barabbas laughed, a masculine interruption into the sanctity of this women's experience. "Of course, a son." He looked down on the infant, now sleeping fitfully in Samantha's arms. She caught Barabbas's eyes.

"His name is Titus," she said, quiet but with force, "big and strong like you."

Barabbas looked deep into her eyes, but for once Samantha neither quivered nor looked away.

"Titus," he said. He leaned close to Samantha's ear, his voice so quiet that only she could hear. "Now I know." With a quick kiss on the cheek and a wink, he strode from the house. "I'm off to celebrate the birth of my new son."

Samantha grimaced at the emphasis Barabbas had placed on the word *my*. Maybe Barabbas knew, and the possibility frightened her more than his drunken attacks. *Protect my son. Please, protect him.* The simple prayer repeated itself over and over in Samantha's heart until she fell into the exhausted sleep of new motherhood.

Chapter Fourteen

It didn't take long for David to find himself neck high in a game of dice. He had the walk and the talk, and, at least for the moment, the money to back him up. Within an hour, his few coins had multiplied.

David's heart soared. This was the life he was meant to live. In a little over an hour, he had gained more money than most people earned in a month of backbreaking labor. With every roll of the dice, the crowd grew until there was a busy roar of laughter in the street. Money changed hands, the wine flowed, and the street game of dice turned into a street party with David as the honored guest.

Hovering over the large pile of coins in front of him, David had a flickering thought: *I should quit now.* But the thought vanished as another roar erupted from the crowd. David laid down a bet and the game continued.

Then the tide turned. The pile of coins began to dwindle, and David found himself laughing less and drinking more. Another loss and David picked up the few remaining coins. He was still ahead, but not by much. He felt the small weight of the coins and shook his head to clear it of stupor. *I can go home now*, he thought, *and tell Samantha I got five pieces of copper for that worn-out cow. I will be a hero in her eyes.* He would even have enough left to buy seed for planting. Samantha would be amazed. The thought gave him the strength to stand up and put the coins in his pouch.

"Where are you going?" The voice boomed in David's ear, and a large beefy hand gripped his shoulder.

David shrugged off the hand and looked directly into the stranger's face. "I have a woman waiting for me." Saying the words out loud made the notion that Samantha would be overjoyed at his return sound plausible. Yes, he needed to go. Already, he had kept her waiting too long.

The man smiled broadly and gripped David's shoulder again. "You won me a lot of money tonight, friend. How about I buy you a bottle of wine?"

Before David could reply, the man steered him to an outside table at a nearby inn. "Wine for everyone," he shouted. "We have a winner among us."

David felt ten feet tall. People cheered and patted him on the back. He smiled and clasped hands with the well-wishers. It no longer mattered that his pile had dwindled. He still had more money in his purse than when he left the auction yards. David's chest puffed out. That afternoon, on the dirty streets of the town of Shechem, David felt

Chapter Fourteen

like a king. He was far from Samantha's house and even further, both in heart and distance, from his own, but it didn't matter. For a few brief moments, he was happy again. He was a winner.

Chapter Fifteen

It seemed to Samantha that Titus changed every day. Before long he was rolling from one side to another and then, in a blink of an eye, he was sitting up and crawling. She delighted in the changes in her young son. Her joy in his innocent sweetness was her only consolation from the dark moods of her abusive husband. Once Samantha had recovered from the rigors of childbirth and was on her feet again, Barabbas began a new game. Though he never outright accused Samantha of foisting another man's child into his household, he insinuated it in every other possible way. His slaps became more frequent and his cunning even more frightening.

Little Titus became both her vulnerability and her protection, her own small Roman soldier. Strange as it seemed, Barabbas never struck her in front of the boy. Samantha found herself carrying Titus whenever Barabbas was anywhere around the house. Fortunately,

Chapter Fifteen

this wasn't often. He had his gang of thieves and his personal philandering. Samantha breathed sighs of relief when he left the house and shivered with fear whenever he returned.

Samantha was not the only woman in the world to despise her husband. She was, however, more honest than most women. Barabbas was her third husband. She had been unprepared for the heartache of her first husband and for the heartbreak of her second. But she had deliberately chosen Barabbas for her own purposes. This was a marriage of necessity, but Samantha daily regretted that decision.

She recalled the stories the elders told of the weak-eyed Leah, the neglected older sister foisted on the handsome Jacob. Strange, how seldom Samantha thought of Leah. Usually it was the beautiful Rachel who captured her imagination. But now her sympathies were with the older sister. How humiliating it must have been for the girl to be forced to dress in the heavy veils that disguised her identity. The shame she must have felt at enduring Jacob's anger when he came face to face with his father-in-law's dreadful treachery. God honored Leah with sons, while Rachel remained barren, but that didn't change Jacob's affections. The elders told how Jacob favored the two sons that Rachel eventually bore, though the younger one cost her life.

Oh, to be loved like Rachel. Samantha usually wasn't given to romantic notions. Any girlish dreams left after Stephen's desertion died with Titus out in the Mediterranean Sea. But this was a dream that never seemed to completely vanish, though for now Samantha found consolation for her grieving heart only in her boy.

Otherwise, she bore her daily regrets with as much dignity as she could. It helped that the family was not destitute. Barabbas provided food, shelter, and clothing for his household, seeing such provision as symbolic of his success in his chosen profession. Sometimes he even gave Samantha gold earrings or silver bracelets. But while she accepted his gifts with feigned joy—how could she do otherwise when his brilliant eyes marked her every expression—she hated the stolen items. And she certainly worked for her keep. Barabbas insisted, and she could not do other than obey his commands.

One hot afternoon, as Samantha tended the garden, Titus managed to stand on two unsteady feet and take a cautious step forward before falling on his bottom. Samantha smiled at his cute efforts and marked the moment in her heart as a small treasure. But the icy fingers of fear gripped her heart. Barabbas was threatening to take Titus with him on his journeys once the boy could walk. She didn't really believe he would. After all, what would he do with a toddler when he had other, more pressing and evil activities to engage in? But she couldn't take a chance. Barabbas couldn't know, not yet, that Titus was beginning to take his first tottering steps.

Samantha reached out her arms to her precious son. He crawled to her and they sat quietly amid the herbs and vegetables. *If only it could always be like this*, Samantha dreamed. *No Barabbas threatening me and my boy. If only Titus hadn't died.*

Chapter Fifteen

Though Samantha continued carrying Titus around as long as possible whenever Barabbas was home, this couldn't last for long. The child had his Roman father's stocky build and it soon became awkward to balance his weight on her hip.

But as Samantha had suspected, Barabbas only laughed the first time he spied Titus walking from the table to his small bed. "I wondered how long you were going to carry that piece of trash," he said, his eyes wet with tears from laughing at his joke. "Do not ever think that I don't know what you're up to."

He pulled Samantha into his lap and she endured his drunken kisses as best she could. But they only lasted a few minutes. Barabbas pushed her onto the floor and stood up. "You're a cold one," he said. "But where would you be without me?" He glared at Titus. "Or that little garbage?"

Once Barabbas was out the door, Samantha coiled into a ball and cupped her hands over her face to protect her from the cold floor. *What had she done?*

In the following months, Barabbas's abuse worsened. He was clever in his meanness and his beatings. He never broke Samantha's arms or legs because then she wouldn't be able to keep the house, cook for him and his thieving companions, or work in the fields. But a bruised face, aching ribs, and a hurting heart were nothing to him. Soon his attention turned to Titus, though he never beat the boy with his fists. Only with his words.

Samantha was trapped in a design she had created. Divorce was not an option. Barabbas made that very clear. In his twisted mind, marriage gave him cachet among his thieving peers. Besides, his sadistic nature enjoyed toying with Samantha as if she were a caged bird whose very existence depended on his brutal nature. Samantha, in shame and fear, began to pray for Barabbas to die.

In a desperate time, Samantha had sought a husband to provide a home for herself and her unborn child. Now she lived with fear as her landlord. Though no bars or locks imprisoned her, she was caught in an escape-proof prison. Other women she knew were serving the same type of life sentence, but Samantha had only enough sympathy to manage her own circumstances. To try to ease the hurt of anyone else would take more energy than she could muster.

It was true, Samantha mused. She lived behind bars no one could see. And delightful, innocent Titus served as her guard. She couldn't leave Barabbas without taking Titus because of her fear of what he would do to her son. She couldn't leave and take Titus with her because she had nowhere to go.

Samantha dreamed of taking Titus back to her mother's hut and living without the constant fear of Barabbas. However, Samantha knew Barabbas would look there first. And she also knew her mother would not welcome two additional mouths to feed. The latest news around town was that a new man now lived with her mother. No. Samantha and Titus would not be welcome.

Some women live in fear of being alone. Some women live in fear of being destitute. Samantha knew those fears. But now she was afraid of being killed. Not that she was afraid to die. However, hell would be to know that Titus was alone with Barabbas. She knew that unless her twisted

Chapter Fifteen

prayers were answered, she was tied to the evil, abusing criminal for life.

Samantha's desperate prayers went from a bedtime ritual to a constant thought stuck in her head like a hopeless mantra: "Die, please die." She silently whispered the words in response to every comment or action Barabbas made.

Of course, he never heard it, but if looks could kill, he died a thousand deaths.

More months passed and Samantha began feeling a strange tingling whenever Barabbas was near. The beatings lessened. The harsh words weren't spoken as often. Something was changing and it frightened Samantha more than the beatings and the abusive words. Then one day, as she washed the dishes, she felt as though scales were ripped from her eyes with a startling insight: "He will kill you."

She didn't know where the thought came from, but she knew its truth in the very depth of her soul. What could she do?

Samantha began sleeping with one eye open, and she put a large stick under her bed. She left the shutters unlocked and placed a small stool within reach to provide an easy escape through the bedroom window.

Barabbas's absences became even more frequent, giving Samantha a much-needed respite from her fears. When his friends came by, Barabbas went outside to talk to them. The new level of secrecy made Samantha extremely uncomfortable. She felt like the end was near and wondered if she should take Titus and make a run for it. But the old question remained: Where could she go that Barabbas wouldn't find her? And if he found her, what might he do in his anger?

One evening, Barabbas lingered after finishing the supper Samantha had so carefully prepared. "Aren't you going out tonight?" she finally asked when he made no move to get up from the table.

Barabbas said nothing. No response at all. He only stared at Samantha until she turned away. But she could still feel his persistent glare piercing a hole through her.

She didn't dare ask him anything else, but quietly went about her chores of cleaning up after the meal. When she reached for his plate, he grabbed her arm in his vise-like grip and pulled her near him.

"You're going out," he said. "You and your brat. I want a divorce."

Samantha didn't know whether to laugh or cry. But that night she began to believe in miracles again.

Chapter Sixteen

IN THE SHORT time it took to go through two bottles of wine, David lost his money and ran up a considerable debt in a game of chance with his generous friend. That friend now wanted to know how David planned to pay the debt.

David was too disoriented to answer. He attempted to walk out when two men grabbed his arms. "Arkadius asked you a question," one of them said.

"Who?"

The other man slapped David across the face. "You'll pay him the money you owe him or you'll work in his field until your debt is paid."

The two men pushed David to the ground and he groaned at the impact. Staring at the dirt, he thought back to childhood scuffles with his older brother. They had never hurt like this. Never before had David felt the sting of someone's hand on his face unless it was the small fingers of a lovely lady. Those were worth whatever caused them. This was different. The taste of blood felt metallic in his mouth and he knew his lip was bleeding.

Thinking of his older brother, David remembered life at home—the land, the cattle, the bountiful table in his father's house. David knew he had made some bad choices in his life, but this was one of the few times he ever admitted it. Why was it so wrong that he didn't like to work in the fields and tend to the animals when there were so many servants who could do those jobs? But right now, David thought field work and livestock were preferable to bloody lips.

The two men snatched him back up as if he were a rag doll. The first man struck him again as Arkadius shouted, "You have a debt to pay."

"I'll pay you when harvest comes." David wiped his mouth on the sleeve of his robe. "I need to go home now. Like I told you before. I have a woman waiting for me." David grinned his most disarming grin.

Arkadius was not impressed. The blow to the stomach caught David totally unaware, and he doubled over in pain. Now he was really frightened. Managing to stand upright, he held his stomach and thought fast.

"I will give you this robe in payment," David offered. It was a fine one, another prized garment from better times.

"Give it to me," Arkadius demanded.

David removed the robe and handed it to the other man. Arkadius examined it and even murmured a comment about the fineness of the cloth and the stitching. Then he tossed it to one of his men.

"It will do," he said, "but only for half the debt."

Chapter Sixteen

"Half?" David spat out the word. "It is worth more than what I owe you. You know it."

"But I say it is not. Are you sure you want to disagree?"

David looked at the two companions who seemed eager for any excuse to hit him again. He looked at his feet and shook his head.

"Our business is settled then," Arkadius announced. "You'll go home after your debts are paid."

The other two men grabbed David by his arms again. He struggled to get free, but found himself once more on the ground. Drifting in and out of consciousness, he then felt himself being loaded into a wagon. Surprising even himself, David thought of God. *I wonder if God knows what's happening to me.*

When David was a boy, his father always talked about God. If he or his brother said, "Thank you, Father," or "You're so wise, Father," his father replied, "I am only a shadow made by the light of God's goodness."

Another recurring conversation seeped into David's consciousness. He remembered his father's smooth voice. "My sons, if you were to ask me for bread, I would not hand you a stone. If you were to ask for a fish, I would not give you a snake. If I, being only human, know how to bless my children, then God, who is divine, must be the greatest of all parents."

David longed for the innocence of those boyhood days. Anything to take him out of this rattling wagon, but instead he felt every bump in the rough road. He feared his ribs might be broken and he knew his pride was shredded. He listened to the conversations of the other men as they slowly covered the miles.

From the talk, David gathered that Arkadius had grown very rich. His employees weren't happy, though, about the meager cash that flowed down to them. David overheard one saying, "Can you believe he's going to build a bigger barn? How much does one man need? He could do a lot of good for the rest of us if he wasn't so stingy."

Another man answered, "Arkadius is like all the rest. All greedy once they make some money. They never get enough and there's always a bigger barn to build."

David coughed to clear his throat, holding tight to his ribs as the effort wracked his body. One of the men turned to him. "You'd better thank God that Arkadius is letting you work. He could have killed you. Mercy must be following you today."

Mercy? This didn't feel like any mercy David had ever heard about. His thoughts drifted again to his father. He remembered the older man saying that mercy and grace came only from God.

"Mercy simply means you are not going to get what you actually deserve," the father had told his boys. "Grace is getting what you don't deserve." He gently laughed as his sons tried to think through the concepts he was teaching them. "Yes, children, it takes God to think of such wondrous things."

Right now, David didn't feel as though God was giving him mercy or grace. He felt beat up, physically and spiritually. He felt shame and regret. And now, his head was amplifying his lament with an aching throb.

Chapter Seventeen

SAMANTHA NEVER KNEW what caused Barabbas to ask for the divorce, but she guessed one of his lovers must have insisted. It didn't matter. He left her that very night with a few coins and a stern warning that she and Titus be gone from his house by the time he returned. Samantha lay awake that night, not in fear, but making plans for her and Titus's future.

Early the next morning, she packed clothes and food in bundles and began the long trek to the temple village perched on the side of Mount Gerizim. The plan had come to her in the night. The coins wouldn't last long and the hopeless truth was that she still needed masculine protection. But she was changing fishing holes. No more dark inns or drunken brawls. Surely she could find a good man at the mountain temple.

Since she had been publicly abandoned, Samantha expected to find acceptance at the temple. Though it wasn't far from her childhood village of Sychar, she had been there only a few times in her life. Her family had made the trip only when absolutely necessary, especially after her father left. As far as her mother was concerned, the temple services were little more than a stage for self-righteous worshippers to perform their piety in front of the community. A place to gossip about who was there and who wasn't and the events that captured the attention of the small circle that was their world.

Samantha thought back to those early trips. In her earliest memory, her father was still with the family on these journeys and he knew all about the history of the temple. Samantha remembered being filled with awe at the mysteries of the shrine. About five hundred years before, the Persian governor Sanballat allowed the Samaritan people to build the temple on Mount Gerizim. If the Hebrews didn't want them in Jerusalem, then they would worship on their own mountain in a temple of their own design. A temple more like the old Mosaic tabernacle.

According to the stories of the temple priest, even the conqueror Alexander the Great at one time gave of his treasury to rebuild the sacred place of worship. But only a century before, Judean armies, in their jealousy and hatred, destroyed the Mount Gerizim temple.

It didn't matter. The Samaritans still worshipped at the mount. The ruins were a reminder of the enmity that existed, that would always exist, between Samaria and Judea. As a young child, Samantha had listened to the temple elders' tales, told around late-night fires, whenever

Chapter Seventeen

she could before one parent or the other shooed her away.

But through the years, the temple lost its aura and became only a building where men with big eyes and critical words ruled over a people enslaved by the desperation of their lives. Samantha's family had never been leaders in the temple community. They were the needy. The only reason she was going back now was because she was needy again. She needed a man.

Once she and Titus arrived at the mountain village, Samantha sought out a suitable inn. After a discreet word with an innkeeper's wife, heated negotiations, and the exchange of a few of her precious coins, Samantha set her small bundle on the rickety table inside a dim room. The hut was small with only two rooms and a tiny courtyard. But it was all she and Titus needed. She hoped her future and that of her son would be more secure before another year's rent was due.

With only a few possessions, it didn't take long for Samantha and Titus to settle into her new home. The cleaning and sprucing up were welcome tasks that took her mind off other worries.

The next morning, Samantha carefully dressed and headed for the temple. As she approached the stoic house of worship, she felt a familiar warmth. Would she be condemned for the mistakes of her youth? Samantha was tired of feeling condemned.

A woman walked toward her and smiled. Samantha's heart turned to fear. Did the woman know who she was? But the woman walked past her and greeted someone else. The two quickly whisked themselves away from

Samantha's presence. When the old woman returned, she frowned at Samantha. *So it has already begun.* Samantha sighed.

Throughout the worship time, she sat upright and stiff on the hard bench in the women's section. From her outward appearance, she resembled the other worshipping women. But inside, Samantha's stomach felt sick. No one talked to her or asked her name. No one was kind enough to give her a greeting. As her trembling hand touched the cold iron door handle to go outside, she heard a voice behind her. "It's good to see you, Samantha."

She turned to see who had broken the silence of the somber place. The dark-haired man was dressed in the robes of a temple priest. His brown eyes were soft and welcoming. "Do I know you?" Samantha asked.

The man gestured toward the door and followed Samantha outside. The people who had been lingering in small groups turned to stare and then scattered as if the building was on fire and they were running for their lives. "Sometimes I feel it's all a waste of time." The man sighed.

Samantha was confused. How odd that he would talk to her. And what did he mean?

"I know who you are," he finally said. The words dropped like stones into a dark ravine, pushing Samantha before them into fear. "You're Samantha of Samaria. I was told of your arrival."

"By whom?"

When the priest mentioned the name of the innkeeper's wife, Samantha realized she had been holding her breath.

Chapter Seventeen

"Oh, yes. She was very helpful." Samantha didn't know what else to say. She was so afraid that her reputation had preceded her, but apparently it was only the gossip of a talkative woman eager to share news of any strangers to the village.

"You are always welcome here," the man said with a smile. Then he turned on his heel and returned to the temple building.

Chapter Eighteen

BUMP. BUMP. BUMP. David's head bobbed against the splinter-filled floorboard of the wagon. Fear washed over him anew as he wondered what would happen to him.

Most of his life, he reflected, had been like this wagon ride, rough, coarse, and in the wrong direction. How often he thought he had a plan, only to find out he didn't know anything. Looking back, he realized he had been on a steady downhill slide since leaving his father's house. For ten years he had been on his own. And now here he was, virtually a prisoner to a debt he hadn't meant to take on.

At first, money had not been a problem. He threw big parties with lots of friends and lots of wine. But as the money slipped through his fingers, the quality of his wine, and his friends cheapened. His friends found new places to be entertained. When the inheritance ran out, David had to find work—the very thing he had left his father's house to avoid.

Chapter Eighteen

It didn't matter to David's father that they had servants and farmhands. The old man required David and his brother to take responsibility for the land and the livestock. How many times had David maneuvered ways to shirk that responsibility?

His father would shake his head and reprimand him. "If you don't learn to work at home, the world will teach you." David only laughed at the dire warnings. Often his father said he had failed his boys. He had been too easy on them, and by being too easy, he had made their lives hard. That only made David laugh more. *Easy?*

But that was then, and now David had a new understanding of his father's words. In fact, every time his throbbing head bounced against the wagon floor, he thought this was the hardest lesson his head had ever felt. Every breath caused a sharp pain in his side and he knew at least one rib must be broken. His nostrils were caked with dry blood and he still tasted blood in his mouth.

What would his father say if he could see his younger son now? David blushed with the shame of imagining his father seeing him in this condition. In his mind, he could see his father's clear dark eyes, usually so youthful and bright, clouded with disappointment and sorrow.

David left his home to be free of the work. But it was deeper than that. He also left to be free of his pompous elder brother. David knew the older son resented him, even blamed him for the death of their mother. But wisdom comes with the clear, stark vision of hindsight. David realized now what a pest he had been, how often he had purposely angered his brother just for the fun of seeing him lose control. And then there was the morning he had left. David grimaced at the memory and tried to shove it back into a dark corner of his mind. But the door cracked and the memory insisted on being relived.

The night before, David had been out with friends. They began mourning the recent death of David's uncle, but as the wine flowed too freely, the mourning became a drunken fest. David woke the next morning in the hay barn. His father kicked at his feet and David remembered his initial fear—dealing with the disappointment of his father. Never had he seen the old man so angry.

The father's trembling voice rebuked David. In his anger, his voice cracked with disappointment and sorrow. The older man stammered to express the shame that David's actions had brought to his uncle's memory and to his father's household.

David jumped up and shouted vile words of derision and contempt. His father grabbed him by his shoulders and shook him violently. However David pulled away from the old man and walked out of the barn. It was the last day he spent in his father's house.

As the wagon hit another hole in the road, David was jolted so hard that he landed sitting up. He folded his arms around his shoulders and prayed that he could feel his father's arms around him again. About this time, he gagged on a foul odor that laid assault to his blood-caked nostrils. The wagon slowed to a stop and David covered his mouth. What was that awful smell?

Again, David's surroundings mirrored the condition of his heart. The stench of David's life was rank and he knew he had finally arrived at his appropriate destination.

Chapter Nineteen

IN THE FOLLOWING months, Samantha took Titus to the temple for almost every worship observance. She soon realized that the priests and worshippers here had their own definitions of right and wrong, their own understanding of absolute truth. In that, they were no different than other temples where she had worshipped.

With an astute insight into human nature born of wariness, Samantha soon realized her favorite priest was completely wrong for his vocation—at least in this temple where the elders disliked him and the women questioned his allegiance to God. But his warmth and kindness touched a cold place in Samantha's heart. To her own surprise, she found herself looking forward to their brief conversations after services ended. Brother Luke told Samantha he had been at the Mount Gerizim temple for two years as an apprentice. Though he didn't complain, Samantha noted the weariness in his eyes.

The other women appeared to Samantha to be annoyed that their holy priest sought out her company. Soon they had the entire village teeming with gossip. As their friendship grew, Brother Luke shared his frustrations with temple politics. He believed God wanted a relationship with his people and Brother Luke found himself surrounded by a crowd that wasn't interested in anything but rules. He believed God was love, forgiveness, and hope, but the elders preached fear, judgment, and condemnation. Samantha found herself warmed by his passionate outbursts and couldn't help feeling a little proud that he shared his thoughts with her.

If the temple elders thought they had groomed Brother Luke into the kind of priest that would keep the fear of God in their people, they were mistaken. Brother Luke revered the Holy Law, but he was searching for the God who burned in his heart. He dreamed of the day he would be an elder and how he could change the mood of temple worship with his understanding of the historical stories of Scripture. People with sin, people with a past, could find God. Samantha felt Luke was offering a cup of hope to her and she wanted to drain it fully.

One afternoon, Luke asked Samantha if he could walk her and Titus home. This was the first step on a new road for Samantha, but, looking back, she realized it was the beginning of the end of Luke's ministry. On that dusty walk to Samantha's house, she fell in love with the holy priest.

The elders called Brother Luke before them. Samantha knew only what she overheard from the gossiping women. He was chastised, reprimanded, and sanctioned to talk only to the men. As the days passed, some people scoffed openly at him, reproaching him for his acceptance of a divorced woman into their holy sanctuary.

Luke stood strong in the face of persecution. With a true love for God, he determined that those with hate and anger would not govern his life. He felt offended by his superiors, abandoned by his flock, and confused about his role in the temple. But he knew he loved God. And he knew he loved Samantha.

With so much hatred directed her way, Samantha quit attending the worship. She became known as Samantha the devil and Samantha the seducer. She noticed that those who were loudest at calling her vile names were the young women. Their jealous hearts couldn't forgive Samantha for gaining Luke's love.

Though Samantha begged Luke to leave, he refused. The harder things got, the more committed Luke became. It began to seem that Luke enjoyed challenging the elders. He lit into the fight of his life, but he lost. However he didn't know it, not then. Samantha could see it all so clearly now. With each passing day, Luke became more ensnared by her love and less enchanted by temple ministry.

In the following weeks, the elders manipulated Luke's personal life. They sent him to other towns on errands or insisted he come alone to various temple functions. In boldness, they challenged him during temple services. Samantha wondered why they didn't just banish him, but the elders seemed determined to teach Luke a lesson. With generations of religious hierarchy behind them, they tormented Luke as slowly as a bored cat toys with a frightened mouse.

From her years with Barabbas, Samantha had learned well the lesson that power is only enjoyed when it is put to the test. Men like Barabbas, like the temple elders, found pleasure in acknowledging the existence of their power over others.

With each new maneuver of the leaders, Samantha grew more disenchanted with the spiritual relationships of the temple elders and their followers. She knew Luke would be forced to choose between her and his calling. She tried to tell him not to choose her, but the more she begged him, the more determined he was to show her his love and loyalty.

What does a man do, she wondered, *when his choice is acceptance or rejection? Love or hate?* Once again, Samantha felt herself moved to prayer. *Let him choose acceptance. Let him choose love.*

Again, Samantha gained wisdom with hindsight. She could see now that, for Luke, the choices were the same. He thought that if he chose Samantha he would be accepted and loved. If he chose the life of a temple priest, he would be accepted and loved. Luke had never recognized that his choice needed to be based on other criteria.

Everyone but Luke could see that Samantha was broken, bitter, and full of home-grown rage. Even Samantha, now that some time had passed, could see that. Luke wanted to be, was determined to be, her savior. He thought he was the man who could redeem her softer side.

Chapter Nineteen

But Samantha ached to have to admit that Luke's inventory of her was a sad exercise in blindness. If love is blind, then Luke was struck by something far more relentless and deep. Somehow he took leave of all of his senses. He was determined to prove that love could change anyone, and he was willing to stake his life to this grand experiment.

Chapter Twenty

"GET TO WORK, you lazy freeloading bum!" David felt a boot strike him in the middle of his back. He fell out of the wagon headfirst onto the ground. An angry-looking man rushed over to kick him again. David got to his feet with awkward movements.

The man halted in front of him and laughed. David looked around, wrinkling his nose at the horrid stench. A pig farm. David turned back to the man. "Who are you?" he asked. "Why am I here?"

The man reached for David, turning him so that he had him by the hair. "You're here to pay your debt to Arkadius."

Another man stood nearby. "You can slop hogs all night," he said, then spat on the ground. "You can leave when the sun comes up."

"I think my rib is broken." David's voice sounded whiny even to him. But that didn't mean he wasn't telling the truth.

Chapter Twenty

"Oh, you have a broken rib, do you?" The man who held his hair slammed his other fist into David's abdomen. "How about now? How many ribs are broken now?"

As the man spoke, David leaned forward and was hit again on the top of his head. The world darkened and he felt his grip on consciousness fading into overwhelming pain. When he woke, a small puddle of blood oozed from his mouth. In the darkness, he could barely see the two men sitting a few feet away from him. As he sat up, he almost knocked over a bucket that had been placed by his side.

The younger of the two spoke first. "If you're not finished by the time the sun comes up, you'll have to stay another day. So unless you like it here, you'd better pick up that bucket and get to work."

David dragged himself to his feet and picked up the weathered bucket. The stench of pigs threatened to gag him, but he tried breathing through his mouth to avoid the smell as much as possible. Across an opening was a huge vat with a swarming cloud of flies above it. As David got close to the vile pool of slop, he lost his stomach again.

The men laughed. "There you go! You've got one bucketful there," one shouted. "You should have given that to the pigs."

"You're going to have a long night, big spender."

As David plunged his bucket into the slop, he felt sick again. Finally his stomach was empty of all its contents and his soul felt just as hollow. His spirit was as broken as his ribs. David couldn't help but think that he finally had hit rock bottom. What a waste his life had been. Always living for the moment, but never planning for a moment like this. He had seen people slop hogs, but he had never done it. The beasts were abhorrent to him. Unclean. And now here he was in the midst of them and their stench.

He remembered a time when he cursed his father's blacksmith for not having his horse shoed on time. His father quietly explained that the blacksmith's arm had been severely injured the day before. "He couldn't do the work, David." His father's voice, as always, was calm and smooth. But David only reacted with anger. "I bet he still eats plenty with one arm."

David recognized now that he was a cruel taskmaster with no compassion for his father's servants. And now he was reaping what he had sown. David realized, in just a small way, that he deserved to be with these unclean animals. He deserved to be the one slopping the hogs. Instead of being repulsed by the revelation, David realized that his aching heart actually felt a little bit of relief.

In every man the spirit yearns to be right with God. Where had that thought come from? Was it something his father had said? David pondered the thought again. *In every man the spirit yearns to be right with God. But sometimes being right is painful and harsh, yet this kind of pain can bring relief to the untouchable parts of a man's spirit.*

Yes. His father had said those words. Often he was speaking to a servant, sometimes to a family friend. Giving wise counsel and comfort to those in need no matter their station in life. Somehow the phrases had hidden themselves in David's mind and heart until this moment. Now, when he needed them most, it was as though his father were saying them directly to him.

Chapter Twenty

While slopping the hogs, David wasn't just paying off his gambling debts. With each painful step, he began paying the debt he owed humanity. He carried bucket after bucket of slop, painstakingly and with aching muscles, to the hogs. In this slow, painful way, David came to terms with the man he was.

The road was hard and he had paved it himself with a lifetime of selfish decisions. Every thought before that night had only to do with what was best for him—what he wanted, what he could have, and how it made him feel. David's life had always belonged only to him, and look where it had led him.

By the middle of the night, his body and spirit were broken. He was tired, hungry, and alone. Feeding someone else's hogs on someone else's farm. David truly was a poor man. Never had he been in such want.

All of David's life, he had sought power, prestige, and attention. He had never hungered or thirsted for anything but pleasure. As long as he had stayed in his father's home, goodness and mercy had followed him. He hadn't known how terrible it is to want, how want causes a person to feel that things are unreachable.

Even now, David had a long list of wants. His list was filled with things that had once been at his fingertips. He wanted rest. He wanted peace. He wanted the pain in his side to go away. He wanted to be whole again in both his mind and his body.

However, now he knew that to possess such completeness, he must become whole in his spirit. Was that still possible?

Chapter Twenty-One

THE MONTH BEFORE Luke's apprenticeship was to end, he showed up at Samantha's door. "It's over," he whispered, his voice breaking. "I've been dismissed."

Samantha drew him inside and put her arms around him. "No," she murmured. "They couldn't do that."

But the elders' decision was final. Luke was now an outcast and no longer had a profession.

A month later, he and Samantha married. But the honeymoon ended almost as soon as it began.

Samantha did not marry the brown-eyed priest with the warm smile and promising career. She married a bitter shell of a man who felt as though the whole world was out to get him. Looking back to those early days, Samantha realized how disappointed Luke must have been in her. He expected a loving and supporting wife, but got a skeptical, wary woman with a cracked spirit. She did love him, at least at first, but the scars and bruises

Chapter Twenty-One

of a lifetime of hurts left little room for love to flourish. Without realizing it, Samantha slipped into past patterns, closing her heart to a different experience.

Both had entered the holy realm of matrimony with the false expectation that they would find wholeness within each other. But the reality about wholeness is that it is never found in other people, but only in God.

This was clearly a union of the broken. In the months that passed between their first meeting and their wedding, both Luke and Samantha had changed. But neither had acknowledged that change in either themselves or the other.

With no avocation, Luke had difficulty finding work. He took on odd jobs from the few brave enough to risk the elders' wrath to hire him. Finally he found a permanent position in a local vineyard.

Samantha felt, though she could not name, Luke's resentment. How could she realize the cause when she was wrapped in her own pain? She watched as the bitterness found a foothold inside Luke. It seemed the tenacious weed grew stronger with each passing day. Samantha knew the stranglehold of that kind of cancer, how anger fed it until it became a poison that seasoned every thought and word.

But what could she do? How could she help Luke rid himself of bitterness when she was choking on it herself? At that time, she was blind to his heartache. But later, she thought she understood at least one small part of it. Luke sacrificed everything because of his love for her. But how had she repaid him? Never had she acknowledged the depth of that sacrifice. Instead, as the months passed, she hid behind self-pity and regret, never celebrating his contributions to their home.

In only a short time, the wary young mother Luke had loved, so desperate for friendship, had been replaced by a cynical skeptic with an anger that could be ignited by the tiniest incident. Though Samantha sometimes recognized glimpses of the mistakes she was making in her relationship with Luke, old habits die hard. She found herself wondering every evening if he would return from the vineyard, wanting him to despite actions that screamed the opposite. Afraid to hope too much that he would, in case he, too, abandoned her.

When he did come in the door, her relief was masked by irritation at the sight of his grape-stained fingers and robe. From the unfaithful Stephen, the secretive Titus, and the cruel Barabbas, Samantha had learned one lesson very well: To keep from getting hurt, a person must keep from being loved.

The days became a quarrelsome routine of Samantha questioning every decision Luke tried to make and complaining about what he did and didn't do. She was cold and cruel, though at the time she didn't realize it. Even her compliments contained a cut. Oh, now, it was all so clear. Now that Luke was gone.

One evening, Luke came home angry from the vineyard. Samantha had not baked bread that day and it was the proverbial straw that broke the camel's back. Luke's shouting words came out in a torrent that first shocked Samantha, then kindled her own fiery temper.

"I wish I'd never met you," Luke shouted. "You ruined my life."

Chapter Twenty-One

Samantha responded with screaming and curses. "You quit because you wanted to." Her voice rose over his. "I never wanted you. I never asked you to love me."

Luke stared at her, and in his eyes Samantha saw the wounds she had just inflicted on his soul. But instead of remorse, the wounds puffed her heart with pride and power.

"You got what you wanted, and now look at us." Samantha gestured around the small house. "Every day the same. Living in a hut that is not our own." She picked up a bunch of grapes from the table and dangled it in front of his face. "This is not your harvest." The grapes dropped to the floor. "You are nothing but a field hand. You don't own a basket or a blade. All you own is a bunch of righteous ideas that we can neither eat nor sell."

Luke let out a primal roar unlike any sound he had ever made. His hurt had come from a place he had never been before. He raised his hand to an awkward position, and for a brief moment, Samantha wondered if he would hit her. Time seemed to stop as she considered his intent. Then she stood straight and time continued. Luke only stared, and before she realized what she was doing, Samantha picked up a creamy tan water pitcher and threw it at his head. Luke ducked, then looked from the broken pitcher back to Samantha, then beyond her.

Samantha turned to see what Luke was looking at. Little Titus sat quivering in a quiet corner, silent tears coursing down his cheeks.

Luke squatted to the floor and held out his arms. Once again, he was the compassionate priest, caring only for the comfort of a hurting person. For a brief moment, he was once again the man she fell in love with. But the flame was too small to survive in Samantha's cold heart. Titus was her son. She should be the one to comfort him. But her feet were rooted to the packed earth. Titus ran to Luke's outstretched arms and found comfort on his shoulder.

It was all so clear now, all these years later as Samantha recalled the screaming incident. Luke was truly called to minister to others. Within his spirit burned a desire to ease suffering and an authentic passion to provide compassion and comfort.

The relationships of the small household changed after that day. Luke and Titus, without meaning for it to happen, forged a bond as Titus's tears and fears pulled love from Luke's hard and bitter heart. Samantha was left out. Alone.

Luke may not have been happy about his marriage, but he could survive off the crumbs of happiness. For now, the young son of a dead Roman soldier would feel all the love Luke could give him. Somehow, this little morsel was all Luke needed to survive Samantha's outbursts.

Chapter Twenty-Two

EVEN THOUGH IT was now past midnight, David knew Samantha wouldn't be worried about him. It wasn't the first time he had stayed away all night. The thought made him sad. Here he was out on some unknown farm slopping hogs and nobody knew where he was. Nobody cared. Nobody worried.

Darkness gripped the landscape. The moon provided only enough light for David to barely see the slop pit and the hogs. The two men who beat him now slept. Three more men had joined them sometime during the late evening hours. All were snoring heavily, oblivious to David's pain. David considered making a run for it, but he knew he wouldn't get far with his broken ribs. He didn't want to risk any more beatings.

As David continued the routine labor, he realized he was hungry. He couldn't help but think of the many banquets held in his father's home. What a spread! Practically every week, his father hosted a feast to celebrate one event or another. The fruits, nuts, vegetables, and meats were abundant. David had never known hunger as long as he was in his father's house. Neither did anyone else. Even the lowliest servant ate his fill at every meal.

When the family was joined by honored guests, his father was the perfect host. He insisted that his sons allow each guest to be served first. When David complained once that he was too hungry to wait, his father had gently reprimanded him: "The last shall be first, David. And the first shall be last." David had only grunted. *Who knew what that could possibly mean?*

David still couldn't explain his father's strange expression, but for the first time in ten years, he realized how much he missed the old man's wise instruction. The hunger in his belly took a backseat to the hunger in his heart to see his father again. Would he ever be able to go home again? Was his father still alive?

Would I be turned away?

David didn't notice his tears until he tasted the wet saltiness on his parched lips. As he stood in the shadowed darkness, sparsely illuminated by the full moon, he gazed into the night sky. *Midnight is exactly what it claims to be*, he thought. *The midpoint between sunup and sundown. The darkest part of the day.*

For the first time in David's life, he had a clear view of his own failure. He had wasted his life and he felt his failure down in the marrow of his bones. He was now firmly convinced that these hogs were his reward for a lifetime of riotous living. Instead of seeing the flaws and mistakes of others, David now saw only his own. *The*

Chapter Twenty-Two

only thing a man sees at midnight is the emptiness of his own soul, he mused, and stumbled under the weight of the insight.

At that moment the wind changed direction, and the reek of the hog pen slapped him in the face. David gagged, then filled his bucket once again.

Chapter Twenty-Three

LUKE CONTINUED TO look after Titus by spending as much time as possible with the young boy. Samantha couldn't help but notice and, though she tried to keep her heart hard and protected from hurt, the small gestures chipped away at the rock. Titus finally had a father. Wasn't that what she had always wanted? Wasn't that the reason she picked out Barabbas and endured his brutality?

And yet, she could not bring herself to share in Luke's love. Her fear of intimacy and abandonment still loomed too large. The inner conflict begged the question, "Did the woman create the circumstances or the circumstances the woman?" But Samantha could not face the implications of even considering that riddle. Not yet.

Each morning, Luke rose early and headed to the vineyard. When he came home, he devoted himself to Titus. He taught the six-year-old to fish, to identify the poisonous plants growing near the stream, and to recognize the signs of an impending storm.

Chapter Twenty-Three

Samantha sometimes watched them when they couldn't see her, torn between jealousy and relief. At night, after Titus was in bed, she mended their garments by the dim light of the oil lamp. Between stitches, she sneaked glances at Luke, trying to guess his thoughts. She noted the occasional longing in his eyes when he looked at her, but she found it hard to give herself to him even as she thanked God that he never insisted on his husbandly rights. Sometimes, she would awake in the night and see Luke standing by the window, looking out at the stars. She knew his heart ached, but she could not find the inner strength to comfort him.

Instead, even as she hated herself for it, Samantha realized the power she had over both Luke and Titus. It was intoxicating, this heady feeling that both frightened and thrilled her. Frightful outbursts that spewed forth left her exhausted, guilty, and self-righteous. Why shouldn't she be the one in control? After a lifetime of catering to one person's whims and then another's, certainly it was her turn to do the ordering about. Abuse or be abused, that was her philosophy.

Life continued for two years with no happiness in sight for the family. Luke worked every day at the vineyard, but once he arrived home, he no longer had the same energy to devote to Titus. Instead of running games and swimming in the stream, Luke often sat on the bank and watched the boy. One morning, he didn't get up. When Samantha shook him, he started. He tried to sit up, but the motion caused him to retch.

"What's wrong with you?" Samantha demanded. "You've got work to do."

Luke struggled again to get up, pushing against the solid platform with one hand while he clutched his stomach with his other. Samantha stood before him with her arms crossed, the dark look in her eyes daring him to fall. Somehow, he managed to stand, though he wavered. He smiled a triumphant smile, then lurched forward.

Samantha caught him, bracing her slim body against his unconscious weight, and eased him onto the mattress. He slumped backward and she felt the heat of his fever when she touched his forehead. "Luke," she whispered, her earlier anger replaced by fear. "Luke?" He muttered a word or two that she couldn't understand, then lay still.

As news of Luke's illness spread through the small village, neighbors who had never exchanged a kind word with Samantha appeared with food and medicines. Even two of the temple elders came and prayed for Luke to recover his health. Samantha was amazed at the outpouring of neighborly assistance and compassion. She had never realized how loved Luke was by others. His kindnesses to them during their troubles, kindnesses Samantha had ignored, were being repaid. Luke was reaping the seeds he had sown.

Whether it was the elders' prayers or the women's medicines, Samantha didn't know or care. Luke's health improved enough for him to sit up and even feed himself. But just when Samantha thought the illness was conquered, it roared back with a vengeance, leaving Luke as weak and helpless as a lamb prematurely born.

For the next two years, Samantha found herself caught in a relentless cycle of rage and sorrow. During Luke's bouts of barely conscious weakness, her heart ached

Chapter Twenty-Three

for him to get better. Even the gossips who despised Samantha marveled, however reluctantly, at her attentive care. She tenderly washed his body and kept his bedding fresh and clean.

But during the weeks of improvement, when Luke could sit and take care of a few of his own needs, Samantha resorted to fits of temper. "It's about time you got up," she scolded the first time Luke managed his first unsteady steps from the bed to a nearby chair. "When will you go back to the vineyards?"

Luke only shook his head. Samantha could see his exhaustion and knew he despised the weakness that kept him housebound. She herself didn't understand why she raged at him. It was as if her relief that he was up again needed some kind of release and her fear of losing him boiled into unreasonable anger.

Then a day would come when Luke could barely stay awake, let alone sit up. And again, Samantha cared for him with every tenderness despite her own exhaustion. The times of planting, growing, and harvesting passed. As Samantha prepared the rocky soil for another season, she realized that Luke's good times occurred less often, while the days of complete bed rest grew longer and longer.

For several months, Samantha had slept on a bedroll on the floor beside Luke's bed. Every evening, she rolled out the thin, straw-filled mattress and every morning, she rolled it back up again and shoved it into a wooden chest. Titus almost always slept on the roof beneath the open skies.

One morning, Samantha awoke with a groan. Her sleep had been fitful, her dreams disjointed and strange.

She sat up and glanced toward Luke. He lay on his back, eyes shut and body still. Too still. Samantha knelt by the bed and touched his face. He opened his eyes for a brief moment, groaned, and turned away. That day stamped itself in Samantha's memory like a metal seal on a piece of soft clay.

As Luke slowly slipped away into an unknown darkness, Samantha felt the enormity of what she was losing press upon her. She stretched an arm across his chest and whispered, "You were the one. And now it's too late."

Luke face contorted with pain and his glazing eyes flickered. His breathing sounded as if his body were drowning. Samantha eased his suffering as best she could as the heavy weight of regret settled around her neck like a stone pendant.

The night Luke died, the smell of ripe grapes hung heavy in the air. Samantha was reminded of the purple stains that were so often on Luke's fingers and robe. How she longed for that again, for that to be the worst thing that could happen. But her longing came too late.

Samantha wrapped herself in her widow's robes and regrets. Now that Luke was gone, she reexamined every minute of their lives together and was overwhelmed with guilt and sorrow. Young Titus was sent to stay with his grandmother, while Samantha tried to pull herself together and face another season of being alone.

Chapter Twenty-Four

THE STENCH OF the pig slop told the story of David's life. Old, leftover food and garbage. Once fit for human consumption but now only good for swine. In the same way, a little dishonesty, a harmless white lie, rebellion, and selfishness had combined in David's heart. His life was a vat of slop and it made him sick.

Always before, he moved on and left someone else to clean up after him. From town to town, woman to woman, job to job. When life got tough or boring or messy, he found new places and new distractions. But now he was trapped by a debt he couldn't walk away from, aching in body and spirit.

As he staggered along the rutted path from vat to hog pen, hog pen to vat, David took stock of his situation and he didn't like what he saw. But for once, he faced the reality without fear and without looking around for someone else to blame.

He let his mind wander back to the earliest days of his memory. Those were happy days, when he felt loved and protected by a doting parent and an older brother. David's mother died shortly after his birth. The grief of that old loss washed over him as if he were once again a little boy. But for once, David didn't shrug it back to a hiding place. Instead he let it settle around him. Then he carefully began to examine its ragged edges. *Did my father overcompensate for her absence?* he wondered. *Was I jealous that my brother had memories of her that could never be mine simply because he was older? Did I fear losing my father, too?*

David pondered the heavy questions as he wrapped his mind around the brutal truth of self-examination. In the wee morning hours of a new day, David tried to form the answers he usually avoided. As he continued the back-and-forth trek, he felt the night air change from a dry stillness into a moist breeze that picked up into a gusting wind. The gusts moaned as they blew against the hog pen as if they taunted David's misery. As the wind increased, David felt the damp clamminess of his sweat and blood-stained tunic. He shivered against the sudden chill.

Another memory of his father shot up from his subconscious. The day David left home, his father tried to hug him good-bye. Still angry and puffed up with selfish pride, David pushed his father's arms away. Now David recalled that moment with the deepest regret. His father hadn't wanted David to leave, but he was willing to hug his rebellious son before he did. What kind of love makes a wise man hug rebellion? David was too

Chapter Twenty-Four

miserable to think of an answer. Instead, he recalled his last look at his father, tears running down the old man's wrinkled cheeks.

"Why did a man I treated so badly love me so much?" David asked the hogs crowded around the trough. But the pigs only snorted and shoved each other in reply.

David's older brother had stood nearby, arms folded and teeth clenched. He said nothing as David swung his bundle onto his shoulders and walked away. But David remembered his father's cry, pleading for him to return: "My door will never close on you, my child." David kept walking. "You can always come home."

Never! David had thought.

He wondered now if his father's offer was still good. After so much time and heartache, could he go home again? He just didn't know. How could he know?

Chapter Twenty-Five

AFTER LUKE'S DEATH, Samantha sold her few belongings. She couldn't stay in the hut that held such deep sorrow. Neither did she want to continue living in Mount Gerizim's temple village. Now that the crisis of Luke's sudden illness and the period of mourning were over, her neighbors returned to their own concerns. Their obligation had been to Luke, but they owed no such duty to the widow who had heaped scorn on him while he was alive.

Though the very idea of moving back with her mother made her skin crawl, Samantha had little choice. She was as much a slave to her financial circumstances as the many other taskmasters that ruled her life. *How long do I have to be needy?* she thought as she made the journey back to Sychar.

The *what ifs* were easy to ask, but so difficult to answer. No, not just difficult. Impossible. If she were

Chapter Twenty-Five

rich, she wouldn't need a husband. If she had money, her worries would disappear. Samantha's thoughts were often occupied with daydreams of another kind of life than the one she had, but they brought her little relief. As the days turned into weeks, she developed an irrational fear of dying. At night, she feared closing her eyes in case she never woke up again. Instead she lay on the thin padding and fought her personal demons.

Images of Luke tormented her. "Why was his death so different from that of Titus's father?" The question nagged and poked, keeping her awake with its jabs. When Titus died, Samantha felt her youth had died with him. But as she opened her eyes to her past, she forced herself to admit how little she knew her Roman soldier. How much of her mourning was for him and how much was for the loss of the dreams she had built up around living a life with him?

But with Luke, there was so much regret. The slowness of his death, the agonizing pain he could not escape, haunted her. As his condition worsened, Samantha had watched his body become a shell. His cold, haunting eyes became empty, void of light, as if he were already gone. With each beat of her heart, Samantha's soul flinched with the pain of *if only*.

Samantha arrived in Sychar with only a few belongings, but a great deal of baggage—the invisible kind that burdens hurting and needy people. How could she have any hope when all her dreams ended in death? For some people, hurt builds up like a boiling pot. Often a hurting person wants to break something, but what did Samantha have left to break? Her inward sorrows transformed into anger at the people closest to her.

Anger was an old companion and, despite her longing for peace, a comfortable response. Almost immediately, Samantha and her mother resorted to an odd competitiveness. The older woman's poor parenting had left her with a huge bull's-eye for Samantha to target. But Samantha's hateful comments always missed their mark. There was no more room in the older woman's soul for someone else's anger to reside. She was a victim herself. Bowed by poverty, she raised her children on her own, forcing them to be independent before their maturity could handle the responsibility.

Whenever Samantha tried to vent her frustrations on the older woman, she was crushed by the mother's sharper tongue or pointed indifference. "I won't be here much longer," her mother would moan. "Then who will you kick around? I'm old and sick; leave me in peace."

Samantha imagined her mother would outlive them all, she was so tough, but the whining self-pity always won out over angry looks and gestures.

That left young Titus. Samantha's frustrations and aches headed his way. She knew she was hurting him with her indifference to his grief over Luke's death. But she didn't know how to comfort him. He pushed away from even the most gentle and flimsy touch. And any words she might have spoken sounded hollow even to her. She was certain Titus would not welcome them.

Samantha watched the inevitable change in Titus's personality from the laughing boy Luke took fishing to the surly adolescent who wanted only to be left alone.

Chapter Twenty-Five

But she felt helpless to stop her raging tongue. The verbal abuse grew worse with each passing day, while Titus became more empty. It seemed to Samantha that he thought by doing nothing he could escape her anger. But if that was his plan, it didn't work. She flew at him for doing nothing and she flew at him when he tried to help. The poor boy couldn't win.

Over the following months, Samantha slowly picked Titus apart until the threads of his person wore thin, like an old coat losing its shape and good only for a rag. The bitterness that Samantha despised in her mother enveloped her own days, and she became worse than her mother had ever been at holding on to old grudges.

Remembering those days—oh, how it ached to remember those days. But they assaulted Samantha and she knew she had to face them. So much hate. So much hurt. So little compassion. If her mother cried, Samantha shed not a tear. If Titus was hurting, then she blocked that hurt with every ounce of her strength. For a few moments, she was not the victim. But the power of being in control never lasted long. It was only a temporary high followed by the deep, piercing thrust of regret and shame. The addictive cycle continued, keeping Samantha, her mother, and Titus in its abusive grip.

Chapter Twenty-Six

Dawn broke on Arkadius's hog farm and David woke to the unfamiliar smell of frying bacon. The delicious aroma drifted into David's consciousness and tantalized his hunger pangs. He opened his eyes and was assaulted by the sloppy dark mud of the hog pen. He had fallen asleep with the pigs and was covered with manure and mud. His empty stomach threatened to retch, but he swallowed hard and settled the queasiness. He washed his hands in the dirty water of a nearby water trough, then climbed out of the pen.

As David approached the other workers, he saw they were cooking a big breakfast over an open fire. David smiled as he rubbed his hands together. "I see you boys almost have my breakfast done," he said.

"You can have all you want after you draw the water," said the man who had first hit David the night before.

Chapter Twenty-Six

David grabbed the bucket and headed for the well. He had once helped his father and brother dig a well and he recalled emptying the buckets of dirt as his father sang:

> *Praise be unto you, our blessed Father.*
> *Praise be unto you, our blessed King.*
> *Hear us, Lord, as we cry out unto you.*
> *Hear us as to you our praise we bring.*

His father often sang as he worked, his voice low and almost a monotone. But what he lacked in flair, he made up for in richness and depth.

It took a long time to dig that well, bucket by bucket. David was too small to hoist out a full bucket of dirt by himself. His brother had grown impatient. "This will take forever a half bucket at a time," he complained.

"Be patient, my son," David's father replied. "We want little brother to know how deep the well is."

Though his father had whispered the response, David heard what he said. He pretended he hadn't, but he spent the rest of the day wondering what his father had meant. Why should David care about the depth of the well? He just wanted to be free from the chore so he could play with his friends.

But later, when David lifted a cup of the clear water from that well to his lips, he remembered his father's words. He thought of how the depth of the well gave him the gift of refreshing cool water to soothe his thirst. His father's simple words sweetened the water from that well for David.

Perhaps that early experience and the hard work of digging the deep well made it so difficult for David to see water being wasted. If someone spilled a cup, he tried to save the spreading water as if it were a child in harm's way. He cringed when people took a sip and poured the remaining water onto the ground. David could not forget the countless buckets of dirt that had to be emptied and how long it had taken for his father's well to yield cool water.

Coming back to himself, David pulled the brimming bucket of water onto the side of the well and carefully balanced it there.

"Hurry up with that water," someone shouted from the cooking fire.

By this time, David was hungry, tired, and wheezing for every breath. He worried about his sore ribs and wondered what other damage had happened inside. He winced with pain as he hefted the heavy bucket and staggered with it to the men sitting at the fire. None bothered to help, but each one had a comment.

"What's the matter? A bucket of water too much for the little boy?"

"Maybe you learned something from those hogs you slept with."

"Maybe he taught those pigs a few new tricks."

The men roared with laughter. When David got close, a filthy man with a ragged beard cleared his sinuses and then spit into the bucket. Wiping his mouth with his sleeve, he grinned. "We're having wine for breakfast, boy."

Chapter Twenty-Six

David controlled his rising anger, too afraid of the men's fists to let it show. He turned to walk away only to have the bucket knocked out of his hands. "Sit down, boy," another of the men said in a loud, sharp voice.

This man, a stranger, placed his hand on David's shoulders and pushed him to the ground. Tears pooled in David's eyes as he watched the thirsty ground devour the spilled water. It was like watching life seep away to see the water disappear. That wasn't why it had been drawn from the well. Not to be poured out, useless, into the dirt.

"What a waste," David muttered to himself. "What a waste."

Chapter Twenty-Seven

SAMANTHA NO LONGER looked for a man. Perhaps that's why one found her. Thomas was rich, but he was also old, bald, short, and fat. His one redeeming feature, besides his wealth, was that he had good teeth. He was proud of those teeth and often leaned back, arms on his hips and his big belly hanging out, smiling as broad as a threshing bowl. His hair came out of his ears, his nose, and over the collar of his shirt. It seemed Big Tom had hair everywhere except on the top of his head. He wasn't much to look at until he smiled that disarming smile with those fine teeth.

Big Tom owned one of the largest markets in the town of Phasaelis, several miles southeast of Sychar. The bustling town, in the southern shadow of Mount Sartaba, straddled the Roman road running north from the metropolis of Jericho. At the Phasaelis crossroads, the Roman highway split into two roads that skirted past

Chapter Twenty-Seven

Mount Sartaba, one on the west side and one on the east side. On the north side of the mountain, the two roads intersected with the major route that began at the Jordan River and meandered northwest to the city of Caesarea and the Mediterranean Sea. Travelers on the Caesarea road always stopped at Jacob's well to water their animals and fill their waterskins with the cold running water from its depths.

On more than one occasion, Big Tom stopped at Sychar on a buying or selling trip from the Mediterranean seaports. On one such trip, Big Tom set up his caravan's tents near the small hut on Sychar's outskirts. Titus, excited at the commotion, ran out of the courtyard to see what was going on. Big Tom spotted him.

"You, boy," he shouted. "Gather sticks for a fire."

Titus ran to do the man's bidding and received a copper coin for his efforts.

Big Tom originally intended to spend only the one night outside Sychar. But when he saw Samantha, the stay lengthened. Samantha knew he asked questions about her and she could guess what the other villagers probably said about her.

But his manner, when he offered her a position in one of the stalls at his bazaar, was polite and courteous. Samantha accepted without hesitation. She was ready to leave Sychar and knew another chance like this one might never come along. When Big Tom's caravan pulled out the next morning, Samantha and Titus were sitting among the bundles of goods headed for the Phasaelis marketplace.

Samantha expected that it wouldn't be long before Big Tom propositioned her, or at least flirted with her. But he never did. In fact, he didn't seem to be interested in flirting with any of the women who crossed his path. As far as Samantha could tell, he had only two flaws: He was cheap and he was a glutton.

His stewards and servants knew better than to expect generosity from Big Tom's pocketbook. "I pay you to sell the food, not to eat it," Big Tom told Samantha. He laughed, but the glint in his eyes told her how serious he was about that policy. She heard from other workers that Big Tom fired anyone who was caught stealing. He gave no second chances.

Samantha worked hard and as time passed, Big Tom gave her additional duties and responsibilities. Caring only for her own welfare, Samantha snitched her way into Tom's heart. She told him about the fat jokes other workers made when he was out of earshot, and she had a keen eye for catching shoplifters. Within a year, she was managing most of the market stalls.

Instead of being repulsed by Samantha's surliness, Big Tom enjoyed her spirit. Never had he seen a woman who could order a man twice her size to get out—and have the man obey! Once Samantha numbered the apples to find out who was stealing them. Big Tom was shocked when she revealed the thief to be one of his oldest employees. The woman had worked for him thirteen years and Big Tom was sorry to let her go. But he stuck by his principles and he rewarded Samantha for her diligence.

Eager for more bonuses, Samantha eventually uncovered a den of thievery in the marketplace, many of

Chapter Twenty-Seven

whom were Big Tom's employees. They had been stealing him blind for years. Of course, Samantha's efforts made her unpopular with the other workers. A few no longer had jobs and even more were imprisoned. But Samantha didn't care. They had shown her no kindness in the past and she saw no reason to seek their friendships now.

The only responsibility Big Tom would not give over to Samantha was the handling of the money. She could take care of everything else that had to do with the market except count the money. Big Tom did this at the end of each day behind a locked door.

The system worked well until a day came when Big Tom, uncharacteristically ill, did not come to the marketplace. A huge order of olives came in, but Samantha didn't have the money to pay for them, and the vendor would not leave the olives without payment. Big Tom realized he needed someone he could trust to help out with the financial side of his business. A few evenings later, he asked Samantha to stay behind at the end of the day.

Samantha was curious about Big Tom's request to stay late. She searched her memory to see if there was anything she had possibly done wrong. Had someone lied to him about her? Did he think she was stealing from him? Her fear and anger spiraled. By the time the last stall closed down, her head ached with worry. Big Tom called her into the money-counting room and motioned to a stool. Samantha sat and folded her hands primly in her lap.

"I need you," Big Tom said. "And you need me. I think it's only good business that we get married."

Samantha looked at him, unable to disguise her surprise. "Married? No. I can't." Her heart fluttered and Samantha thought she was going to be sick.

Big Tom never took his eyes off her face. "It's like this," he finally said. "I won't trust anyone with my money except my wife." He let the words float into the air, then continued. "And I need someone I can trust to help with the money."

Samantha met his gaze and searched for something in the depths of his eyes to guide her. She wasn't sure what she was looking for, but she didn't see anything there to cause her any alarm. The words settled into her brain and she considered Big Tom's offer. *A wife to trust with his money*. "Yes," she stammered. "I can do that."

"Good." Big Tom slammed a beefy hand on the nearby table. "The priest is waiting."

"Now?"

"Is there a better time? Of course now."

Big Tom and Samantha married that very evening. They worked during the day, said their vows that night, and slept in separate rooms in the apartment above the marketplace stall. Over the next year, Big Tom slowly turned over the money accounts to Samantha. He taught her to handle the receipts and keep track of the various vendors and suppliers. She learned quickly and enjoyed the challenge.

Samantha's proficiency with numbers filled her with pride, and she knew Big Tom was pleased that she had accepted his proposal. Samantha became so good with the accounting that she could misplace a drachma right under Big Tom's nose and even he would never know. *It's*

Chapter Twenty-Seven

the greedy thieves, Samantha thought, *that get caught*. She couldn't say why she violated Big Tom's trust with her pilfering. Somewhere deep inside her soul she still felt the need to look after herself. Big Tom's kindness didn't seem enough to fill that empty, aching void.

During the first months of their marriage, Big Tom came to appreciate Samantha even more. Though she considered the marriage to be a strict business arrangement, she picked up on the tell-tale signs that Big Tom was beginning to think of her as more than a business partner. He enjoyed talking to her and she realized that they spent more of their evenings in conversation.

Two years later, Samantha's mother died. Samantha joined the other mourners, but her grief was only another bundle to add to her heavy load of emotional baggage. If the woman had been ill, she had hidden it from her daughter. Samantha believed her mother simply wore out with years of unhappiness. Bitterness and anger finally buried her deep within the ground. Perhaps it was for the best.

Big Tom paid for Samantha's mother's funeral. Samantha was overwhelmed by his generous assistance to her family and thanked him by embellishing a new wool outer tunic with fine embroidery and long, thick fringes. Big Tom's grip on his money loosened. He bought new clothes, new furniture for their home, and even a donkey just for Samantha. Now she could ride in style from their large home to the marketplace stalls and back again. It was Big Tom who insisted that Samantha keep her mother's house. "Never turn loose of a piece of ground," he told her. "Our Lord isn't making any more."

Even with Big Tom's generosity, Samantha continued embezzling small sums. She wasn't sure if it was the thrill of tricking someone with Big Tom's reputation for shrewdness or just a bad habit. She justified her thievery by putting in extra time at the stalls or making an extra effort to locate Big Tom's favorite foods. Sometimes she slipped money to Titus, always with a warning. "This is just between you and me," she said. "Never tell Big Tom."

Titus was now a young man with dreams and ambitions of his own. He gladly took the money Samantha offered him, even if it often wasn't as much as he would have liked. She kept a strict limit on what she took, as if her restraint somehow justified her misdeed.

In time, Samantha had little to complain about in her life with Big Tom. For the first time in her existence she was well clothed, had a sturdy roof over her head, and wasn't hungry. But she didn't feel loved. She knew Big Tom adored her, but it wasn't the same. What kind of man was he that not once in their married life had he ever tried to sleep with her? She knew she was still attractive. In fact, now that she ate well and had lost her scrawniness, she was probably the most attractive she had been since the first time she was a bride.

Samantha began dropping hints and making little suggestive overtures. But her womanly charms didn't seem to affect Big Tom at all. One day, Big Tom came home to find Samantha sitting on his bed wearing a thin silken wrap. "I've been waiting for you," she said, keeping her voice soft and warm.

Chapter Twenty-Seven

"Sorry, honey," Big Tom said. "You'll have to keep waiting." He left the room.

Hurt and angry, Samantha returned to old habits. From that day on, Big Tom could do nothing right. She griped and picked fights over silly issues. One evening, after working at the stalls on what must have been the hottest day of the year, Samantha lost all patience and good sense. When Big Tom refused to respond to her nagging, her anger turned to white hot rage.

"Aren't you a man?" she shouted. "Why won't you have me?"

Big Tom looked at her and then down at the floor, deep in thought. When he spoke, his warm voice was tinged with just a hint of ice. "I won't sleep with you because of who you are."

Samantha stepped backward and held up her hands as if fending off a blow. The thought entered her mind that she would have preferred a slap to those hurtful words that reminded her of a sordid past she tried every day to forget. Blinking back hot tears, she retorted, "I'm your wife. Every man makes love to his wife."

When Big Tom spoke, his voice cracked. He cleared his throat and began again. "You are a thief." His quiet voice resonated in the space between them. "I can't love you because you steal from me."

Samantha started to deny the charge, but Big Tom stopped her. "I've waited so long for you to be honest with my money so that I could make it *our* money. I knew that if you truly loved me you wouldn't steal from me."

Faced with the truth of her dishonesty, Samantha sat on the stool and hid her face. But she couldn't shut out Big Tom's words.

"You should have known that I count every penny. I knew every time you took even a half-shekel. It broke my heart to see how easily you could lie to me, Samantha. How could I trust you with my heart?"

Samantha raised her face to him, determination in her eyes. "I'm leaving. I want a divorce."

For the first time in her life, Samantha left a man before he could leave her. And this time she had someplace to go. But she found no solace in either reality.

Chapter Twenty-Eight

David sat at the table of his enemies, but he didn't feel like the legendary King David after whom he was named. As the weathered men slopped hog brains and eggs onto crude wooden trays, their conversation turned to the exploits of a local criminal, evidently a friend of one of David's cruel taskmasters.

"He killed a tax collector," said one.

"Then he will hang from the gallows," said another.

"Not Barabbas," a third joined in. "He always escapes his captors. He'll find a way out of this scrape."

The first man shook his head. "Not this time. His fate lies with Pontius Pilate. He will hang for sure."

As David listened to the men, he realized some of them were glad that Barabbas was in prison, while others seemed to revere the murderer. Being executed was hardly an honorable way to die, but honor among thieves was complicated. Trouble seemed a kind of trophy to some of the men. The wounds and scars of their lives were their medals for a job well done. As some of the men told tales of Barabbas's adventures, David gave silent thanks that he had never met the man. He wished he could say the same thing about his current companions.

By now, David was sober and clear-headed. The wine he had drunk had been released through his sweat and tears. But his tunic reeked of the foul stench of blood and slop and hog manure. He couldn't escape it.

He stood up slowly and looked around to see if anyone was paying attention to him. The men were engrossed in their conversation and the food. David drew another bucket of water. Carefully, he pulled off his tunic and began washing his body. His muscles ached and he still worried about his ribs. But the water was cool and clean and felt good against his bruised skin.

As he dipped the garment in the water, he longed for a cleansing swim in a shaded stream. He wrung out the shirt against his chest so that the water ran down in small streams to his stomach. David wasn't just washing mud and vomit from his body. He was also trying to wash off ten years of shame, rebellion, and sin from his spirit.

"Come clean," he whispered. "Come clean." He was examining his dirt-streaked arms and hands, but speaking to the deep places in his soul. David scrubbed until his chest felt raw. He dipped his arms into the bucket to rinse off the dirt and blood. The murky water turned even grayer and bits of debris floated to the surface. After his best efforts, he stood in a sun-drenched spot and lifted his face to the heavens. He was still dirty, but he felt a little cleaner.

Chapter Twenty-Eight

David returned to the men at the fire and sat down. Now that manure and blood no longer filled his nostrils, he sniffed the aroma of the food. The smell of the bacon was especially tantalizing. The Law forbade the Jewish people from eating pork. David had broken many commandments, but never the ones concerning food. He felt a little funny as he watched the other men enjoying the meat. But he was too hungry to be very concerned about religious laws today. He reached for a slab of the bacon.

One of the men slapped him. "Wait until we're through."

David drew back his hand and watched the men. *They eat like pigs*, he thought. *They smell like pigs.* Amused by his own small joke, David felt pride surge through him. "I've never eaten anything unclean before," he blurted out. "But I'd make a wager that this old pig is surely the cleanest thing at this fire." He laughed and looked around at the others, expecting them to join in the joke. Instead they glared at him, and it slowly dawned on David that his mouth had once again gotten him into trouble.

The nearest one grabbed David by his collar and stood up, pulling David up with him.

"I meant no disrespect," David said. "I was just talking."

It was too late. The man who grabbed David now pulled his arms behind his back. The others took turns hitting his face and stomach. David felt his nose break and his eyes begin to swell shut. Barely conscious, he struggled to breathe and tasted the blood trickling down his throat from his flooded nasal passage. His ribs were numb and he struggled to draw a breath. *I'm dying*, he thought. *They are going to beat me to death.*

David, passing in and out of consciousness, felt his body rise up. Then he felt nothing, as if suddenly he had taken flight. He didn't know if the men had turned him loose or if he were dead. But as quickly as that thought materialized, he hit the ground. The thud was sudden and rude. Lying face down, broken, beaten, tired, and hungry, David realized he was back in the hog pen.

The mixture of blood and mud clogged his nostrils and David felt he was drowning. With a last effort, he tilted his head so that the corner of his mouth found air. Only then did he allow the blackness to swallow him.

Chapter Twenty-Nine

Samantha moved into her mother's old home in Sychar, but regret followed her. The certificate of divorce was settled quickly enough due to Big Tom's influence and capacity for placing coins into the right hands. Samantha already had her own plans. She confided them to Titus.

"We can go to Sebaste," she said, her voice pitched high with excitement. The city, located about thirty-five miles north of Jerusalem, meant a new beginning. "They say the round towers of the city gates are magnificent."

Titus looked away and Samantha tried again. "The bazaar is renowned throughout the region. Think of the business we could have."

"No." Titus shook his head. "I won't go with you."

Fear and anger rose, each emotion fighting for dominance, into Samantha's throat. "Why not?" she demanded.

"I have plans of my own," Titus said. "I'm going to Caesarea."

At the mention of the seaport, Samantha thought she was going to be sick. She took a deep breath. "Why Caesarea?"

Titus shrugged. "I want to."

No amount of pleading, no angry tantrums could change Titus's mind. He accompanied Samantha to Sychar, but left early the next morning. Samantha watched him go and wondered at the strange fate that lured Titus to his father's city. She had never told him the truth about his father and saw no reason to do so now. She just watched him until he disappeared into the horizon.

Before long, Samantha settled into a daily routine. Though it took time for her to think of the house as belonging only to her, the thought brought her peace and contentment. A house without a man! What bliss! And yet the thought always brought a pang as she wondered about Titus. Now other difficulties required her attention. The house needed a thorough cleaning and repairs, the roof needed patching, and the garden needed tending. But Samantha wasn't afraid of hard work.

To earn money, Samantha baked specialty breads for the other townspeople. She had picked up the skill when married to Big Tom and knew she had a knack for it. That was how she met David, the handsome high roller who came to town with money to burn. He was a good customer for Samantha, ordering multiple loaves to feed his feasting guests, and he didn't mind paying more for the bread than the usual prices.

Chapter Twenty-Nine

Only once did David speak to her: "Why don't you come to the feast tonight?" He smiled broadly, a hint of lasciviousness in his eyes.

"I'm not one of your whores," Samantha snapped back.

"I've heard rumors."

Samantha ached to slap the smirk from the man's handsome face. But his business was too important to lose her temper now. "Do you want any bread or not?" she asked, keeping her voice as businesslike as possible.

"The usual." David winked, then strutted away, whistling a jaunty tune.

It was all Samantha could do to keep from throwing a loaf of bread at his backside.

Samantha watched from a distance as David, the prince of pleasure, threw his money around. At first he was the toast of the town, then the town drunk, and eventually the town joke. He moved from his rented palace to a large house, then to a hut. Before long, he was sleeping in the loft of someone's barn. He finally married a village girl, though the marriage didn't last very long.

One day, David showed up at Samantha's garden as she was hoeing the weeds from the tender plants. "Remember me?" he called out to her.

Samantha looked up and shaded her eyes against the harsh sun. "You owe me for bread," she said, then returned to her hoeing.

"I do?" David strode toward her. "I thought all my debts had been paid."

"Not that one."

David positioned himself in front of Samantha, blocking her path and forcing her to look at him. "No one makes bread like you," he said. "I haven't had anything to eat in more than a day. There's nothing I'd like better than a slice of your bread. Maybe with some cheese?"

"How will you pay?"

David looked around at the small property. Samantha could tell he was appraising her ability to keep it up.

"I could fix some things around here."

"You?" Samantha scoffed.

"I have some skills. Besides, I know you don't have a man. You need someone like me."

Samantha winced at the slap of his words and her forehead crumpled into an angry scowl. "I don't need any man." The words barely escaped through her clenched teeth. "You just need to pay your debts."

David backed up a step. "I didn't mean it like that. The truth is, I need you." He grinned the disarming grin that so often got him what he wanted.

But Samantha wasn't charmed.

He grimaced, then held out his hands in a pleading gesture. "If you'll let me stay in your stable, I can work off what I owe you. Please? I'm only asking for a bit of food."

The apparent humility did what the grin had not. "Only today," Samantha said and handed him the hoe. She walked briskly back to the house and left David to finish the garden work. A few minutes later, she returned with a small tray of bread, cheese, and fruit. To her surprise, David had done more in those few minutes than she could have accomplished in an hour.

Chapter Twenty-Nine

David stayed the night and the next and the next. He milked the cow, hoed the garden, and did other chores around the place while whistling a strange little tune. For a time, he lived in the stable, but as the weather changed and the first chill nipped the air, he crawled into Samantha's bed. Tired and lonely, she didn't resist him.

Samantha could not explain even to herself why she allowed David to move from the stable to her bed. He was incredibly handsome, even more so than her beloved Roman soldier. She felt an odd sense of disloyalty at making the comparison. But that wasn't the reason. Perhaps there was no reason except that she was her mother's daughter. She was living in her mother's home, living her mother's life all over again.

David offered marriage, but Samantha refused. In her mind, this was another business arrangement. David worked, though not with as much zeal as before, and Samantha found herself losing customers as the villagers gossiped about her living arrangements.

Samantha and David argued often, but in the dark of night, they clung to each other. It seemed both were too fearful to face life alone again. They slipped into a routine that neither one knew how to escape.

One evening David came home drunk and demanding dinner. Samantha was furious that he spent their last coin on wine instead of the seed they needed for the garden. Not only that, but David had neglected the cow that morning. The milk had been little enough before, but now her bags were empty. She would have to be sold.

That night, the argument escalated. Samantha threw a lamp, brimming with oil, at David's head. He ducked and the lamp hit the clay wall, then fell in pieces to the floor. The precious oil spread into trickling rivulets and thin pools. David stalked out of the house to sleep in the stable. Spent with anger and frustration, Samantha threw herself onto the hard bed. Regret washed over her and, for the first time in years, she cried herself to sleep.

Chapter Thirty

"GIVE ME A drink." That was what the stranger said. But why? Samantha didn't know.

She knelt on the ground, the events of her life, her marriages, and her troubles flashing before her in quick succession. But nothing in her experience had prepared her for a moment like this.

The stranger simply sat and waited. He seemed to know when Samantha had finished stringing together the broken pieces of her past.

"If you knew the gift of God," the stranger said, "and who it is that asks you for a drink, you would have asked him and he would have given you living water."

Her lips felt dry and parched. "Sir, give me this water so I'll never be thirsty and never come here to draw water again. I perceive you are a prophet." Samantha's mind raced as she tried to grasp what was happening to her. She didn't want to talk about her husbands, not to anyone and certainly not to this man. She gazed into his clear eyes. "Our fathers have worshipped on this mountain for generations," she said, gesturing toward Mount Gerizim. "Yet you Jews say we should worship in Jerusalem."

"Woman, believe what I'm saying." The stranger's confident voice cooled the air. "The time is coming when you'll worship neither at this mountain nor at Jerusalem. For God is spirit, and those who truly worship him must worship in spirit and in truth."

"When the Messiah comes, he will explain everything."

"I am the Messiah."

Samantha stared at the homely face and knew he revealed truth to her. She nodded, only slightly, and felt the stone in her chest begin to crack.

The sound of chattering voices distracted her and she looked toward the group of men coming toward them. They noticed her, too, and their talking ceased.

Chapter Thirty-One

DAVID GRADUALLY REGAINED consciousness to a world silent except for the grunting of the pigs. Every muscle and joint in his body ached. The noon sun targeted hot rays directly onto his brokenness. He was alone.

It hurt to breathe. It hurt to move. *Home.* It was all David could think of. He had wasted his life in riotous living, but he had enough. Broken and hungry, he longed for the comfort of his father's arms and the bounty of his father's table. The hunger stabbed him through the other aches and pains. He was hungry enough that even the pig trough filled with slop tempted him. At that moment, he knew what he needed to do. Even his father's hired servants lived better, ate better, than this. He could not return as a favored son of the house, but surely his father had compassion enough to hire him as the lowliest of his servants. He could work hard. He knew he could. And in that way, perhaps he could earn his father's trust again.

David slowly raised himself from the ground, determined to return to his father and to beg for forgiveness. His only fear now was that his father might have died during his absence. In that case, he knew he was truly lost and alone. Once again, David went through the laborious task of washing himself as best as he could. Slowly he began the long walk back to Samantha's house. He owed her a decent good-bye.

As David hobbled into Sychar, he heard a commotion. The villagers stood in a group and someone was shouting. It was Samantha's voice and, for a moment, David's heart turned to ice. What were the villagers doing to her?

He pushed his way through and saw Samantha in the villagers' midst, waving her hands over her head. "Come see a man who told me all the things I ever did," she shouted. "He is the Christ. He is the Anointed One."

The Christ? The Anointed One? David shook his head. *What could Samantha be talking about?* The villagers listened in wide-eyed amazement. "At Jacob's well," Samantha pointed toward the path. First two men, then others, scurried that direction, followed by women and children. In only a few moments, Samantha stood alone, but isolation no longer weighed upon her shoulders. She looked at David, and he thought her radiant smile to be the most beautiful sight he had ever seen. Before he could say a word, her slender fingers gingerly touched his broken face. "What happened?"

"It doesn't matter." David clasped her hand. "What's happened to you?"

"I have seen him." Samantha's eyes were lit with brilliance. "I have seen the Christ! I have tasted water from a well that never runs dry."

Chapter Thirty-One

"The Christ?" David stared at her in disbelief. "Can it be true?"

"Oh, yes. You must come." Samantha grabbed his arm.

David pulled her back and looked deep into her shining dark eyes. Never had she looked so lovely, so pure. His thoughts whirled with emotion and wonder. But then he shook his head.

"Samantha, about the cow," David began. "I got to the auction late . . ."

"It doesn't matter."

"The coins. I gambled and . . ." David's voice broke. On the walk back to the village, he had rehearsed different stories, hoping to find one that would bring pity rather than scorn. Now, he feared the truth would dim the joy he saw in Samantha's face. But the truth was all he had left to give her. "I am so sorry." For the first time in his life, David uttered that simple phrase with honesty and conviction.

"I don't care about the coins or the cow." Samantha looked deep into David's eyes. "I have seen the Messiah. He knew all my pain. You must see him, too."

"No, Samantha." David grasped both her hands firmly in his. "I must go home. Back to my father. I need to seek his forgiveness for all the pain I caused him before I see the Christ."

Samantha considered David's words. For a moment, they stood in silence. Then she nodded, "Yes, David," she said. "You must return to your father. Today, I have returned to mine. Today, I looked into the eyes of God and found what I've been searching for all my life."

Chapter Thirty-Two

Samantha's smile turned shy as she and David walked back to the simple hut. "My entire life I've looked for love. I thought I could get it from a man. But today I found it in myself. The beauty of God is allowing me to see myself. Once I saw myself, I knew what was missing."

"You are beautiful, Samantha," David said. "You always were."

Samantha responded to the compliment with a sweet smile. Then she grew serious. "David, I've blamed you for my unhappiness. But I've always been unhappy. Standing at that well, I thought through my entire life. From my earliest memory of waiting for a father who would not come back to his family to the emptiness of the bed when you didn't come back last night. All my life I've been waiting for a man to rescue me. But today God showed me that I can be whole alone. God was the missing piece

Chapter Thirty-Two

to my puzzle. That's why a man could never fit. The hole in my life was too big for any man to fill. It was so big that it took God to fill it."

The words continued to spill out. Before he left, Samantha had to make him see what she had experienced. She had to share the bliss of new hope and forgiveness with him before he returned home. "You have the same hole, David. You've tried different things, but your need is the same. All your life you've tried to be important. To buy friends. To be popular. The only one who didn't like you to begin with was yourself."

David flushed with the warmth of Samantha's healing words. "You're right, Samantha. I left home to be somebody when I already was somebody."

At Samantha's house, David washed up and changed his clothes. He put together a small bundle of his belongings, and Samantha packed provisions for his journey. When he was ready to leave, they embraced. David tried to apologize again, but Samantha only shook her head. "We hurt each other," she said. "Every chance we could. Perhaps if we had met at a different time . . ." Samantha's voice sounded wistful. David kissed her on her forehead. "Perhaps," he whispered.

Just before he walked out the door, Samantha handed him a waterskin. "Fill it at Jacob's well."

"I will," David said. "I promise."

As he walked from the hut to the path, Samantha climbed the rickety ladder, forgetting for once to curse the broken steps. She stood on the roof and watched as David walked away from the village and out of her life.

He turned once and waved. She raised her arm in farewell.

And then he was gone.

For the first time in Samantha's life, a goodbye came without a sting. Her heart didn't hurt at the sight of David walking away. She was right with herself and that gave her a new place to stand in life. She could finally stand alone.

Samantha of Samaria had met the Messiah at Jacob's well. The well of living water was a well of help. A well of hope. She could truly say she was a different person than the woman who walked alone to draw her water. With David's departure, she was still alone but she wasn't lonely. Alone can be a fine and refreshing place when a person is whole. Samantha of Samaria drank the living water that was offered her and was never thirsty again. Her thirst for love was quenched from a well that never runs dry.

Though Samantha never saw David again, she often wondered what happened to him. In her daydreams, she saw him walking the long road home. And when David finally arrived, weary and repentant, his father stood waiting with open arms to embrace his beloved son.

A Note from the Author

ALL OF US need an encounter with the man at the well. Maybe we have not been married five times, or perhaps we have not wasted all we have on riotous living. Nevertheless we all struggle in some way. This means that even if we are not the woman at the well, or the prodigal son, we still need God.

This is the Good News that is the Gospel. This is the truth that is relevant to all generations: God loves us and our failures are not fatal. No matter how lost we are or how far we have fallen, there is hope in Jesus Christ.

—Pastor John R. Ramsey

The Prodigal Son
As Written in Luke 15:11–24

AND HE SAID, "A certain man had two sons: And the younger of them said to his father, Father, give me the portion of goods that falleth to me. And he divided unto them his living. And not many days after the younger son gathered all together, and took his journey into a far country, and there wasted his substance with riotous living. And when he had spent all, there arose a mighty famine in that land; and he began to be in want. And he went and joined himself to a citizen of that country; and he sent him into his fields to feed swine. And he would fain have filled his belly with the husks that the swine did eat: and no man gave unto him.

"And when he came to himself, he said, How many hired servants of my father's have bread enough and to spare, and I perish with hunger! I will arise and go to my father, and will say unto him, Father, I have sinned against heaven, and before thee, And am no more worthy to be called thy son: make me as one of thy hired servants.

"And he arose, and came to his father. But when he was yet a great way off, his father saw him, and had compassion, and ran, and fell on his neck, and kissed him. And the son said unto him, Father, I have sinned against heaven, and in thy sight, and am no more worthy to be called thy son.

"But the father said to his servants, Bring forth the best robe, and put it on him; and put a ring on his hand, and shoes on his feet: And bring hither the fatted calf, and kill it; and let us eat, and be merry: For this my son was dead, and is alive again; he was lost, and is found. And they began to be merry."

The Woman at the Well

As written in John 4:7–29

THERE COMETH A woman of Samaria to draw water: Jesus saith unto her, Give me to drink. (For his disciples were gone away unto the city to buy meat.) Then saith the woman of Samaria unto him, How is it that thou, being a Jew, askest drink of me, which am a woman of Samaria? for the Jews have no dealings with the Samaritans.

Jesus answered and said unto her, If thou knewest the gift of God, and who it is that saith to thee, Give me to drink; thou wouldest have asked of him, and he would have given thee living water.

The woman saith unto him, Sir, thou hast nothing to draw with, and the well is deep: from whence then hast thou that living water? Art thou greater than our father Jacob, which gave us the well, and drank thereof himself, and his children, and his cattle?

Jesus answered and said unto her, Whosoever drinketh of this water shall thirst again: But whosoever drinketh of the water that I shall give him shall never thirst; but the water that I shall give him shall be in him a well of water springing up into everlasting life. The woman saith unto him, Sir, give me this water, that I thirst not, neither come hither to draw.

Jesus saith unto her, Go, call thy husband, and come hither. The woman answered and said, I have no husband. Jesus said unto her, Thou hast well said, I have no husband: For thou hast had five husbands; and he whom thou now hast is not thy husband: in that saidst thou truly.

The woman saith unto him, Sir, I perceive that thou art a prophet. Our fathers worshipped in this mountain; and ye say, that in Jerusalem is the place where men ought to worship.

Jesus saith unto her, Woman, believe me, the hour cometh, when ye shall neither in this mountain, nor yet at Jerusalem, worship the Father. Ye worship ye know not what: we know what we worship: for salvation is of the Jews. But the hour cometh, and now is, when the true worshippers shall worship the Father in spirit and in truth: for the Father seeketh such to worship him. God is a Spirit: and they that worship him must worship him in spirit and in truth. The woman saith unto him, I know that Messiah cometh, which is called Christ: when he is come, he will tell us all things. Jesus saith unto her, I that speak unto thee am he.

And upon this came his disciples, and marvelled that he talked with the woman: yet no man said, What seekest thou? or, Why talkest thou with her? The woman then left her waterpot, and went her way into the city, and saith to the men, Come, see a man, which told me all things that ever I did: is not this the Christ?

To order additional copies of this title call:
1-877-421-READ (7323)
or please visit our Web site at
www.winepressbooks.com

If you enjoyed this quality custom-published book,
drop by our Web site for more books and information.

www.winepressgroup.com
"Your partner in custom publishing."

Contact the author:

John R. Ramsey
3238 E. Hwy 390
Panama City FL, 32405

pastorjohnramsey@gmail.com

samanthaofsamaria.com